THE 48 LAWS OF SALES

Rodney T Harris II

The Next Step Sales

Copyright © 2024 The Next Step Sales

All rights reserved

ISBN-13:9798326095947

No part of this book may be reproduced, or stored in a retrieval system, or transmitted in any form or by any means, electronic, mechanical, photocopying, recording, or otherwise, without express written permission of the publisher.

CONTENTS

Title Page
Copyright
Introduction
Purpose of the Book   1
Part ONE the fundamentals of sales   4
Law 1: Know Your Product Inside Out   5
Law 2: Understand Your Customer   9
Law 3: Build Genuine Relationships   13
Law 4: Master the Art of Listening   17
Law 5: Always Be Closing   21
Part TWO Advance Sales Strategies   27
Law 6: Solve Problems, Not Push Products   28
Law 7: Adapt to Customer Needs   32
Law 8: Focus on Quality, Not Just Quantity   36
Law 9: Develop a Consistent Sales Process   39
Law 10: Be Passionate About What You Sell   43
overview of Advanced Sales Strategies   46
Part THREE: Building Trust and Transparency   49
Law 11: Be Transparent with Clients   50
Law 12: Be Honest in All Dealings   53
Law 13: Focus on Building Trust   56

Law 14: Maintain Professional Integrity	59
Law 15: Handle Objections Professionally	62
Overview of Building Trust and Transparency	65
Part FOUR: Communication and Persuasion	68
Law 16: Tailor Your Sales Pitch	69
Law 17: Use Storytelling to Engage	72
Law 18: Create a Sense of Urgency	75
Law 19: Emphasize the Value Proposition	79
Law 20: Use Psychological Principles	82
overview of Communication and Persuasion	86
Part FIVE: Emotional Intelligence and Interpersonal Skills	90
Law 21: Develop Emotional Intelligence	91
Law 22: Manage Stress Effectively	94
Law 23: Cultivate a Positive Mindset	97
Law 24: Enhance Your Presentation Skills	100
Law 25: Adapt Sales Strategies to Customer Types	103
overview of Emotional Intelligence and Interpersonal Skills	107
Part SIX: Negotiation and Closing	111
Law 26: Negotiate Win-Win Solutions	112
Law 27: Always Follow Up	116
Law 28: Recognize Buying Signals	119
Law 29: Overcome Price Objections	123
Law 30: Be a Consultant, Not a Salesperson	127
overview of Negotiation and Closing	131
Part Seven: Sales Planning and Organization	135
Law 31: Stay Organized	136
Law 32: Practice Effective Time Management	139

Law 33: Set and Review Goals Regularly	143
Law 34: Prepare for Every Scenario	147
Law 35: Manage Your Sales Pipeline	151
Overview of Sales Planning and Organization	155
Part eight: Leveraging Technology and Trends	159
Law 36: Utilize Technology Effectively	160
Law 37: Keep Learning and Evolving	163
Law 38: Leverage Trends	167
Law 39: Understand Pricing Strategies	170
Law 40: Measure Your Performance	174
Part nine: Customer-Centric Sales	177
Law 41: Prioritize Customer Satisfaction	178
Law 42: Offer Exceptional Customer Service	181
Law 43: Educate Your Customers	183
Law 44: Utilize Customer Feedback	186
Law 45: Enhance Customer Experience	189
overview of Customer-Centric Sales	191
Part Ten: Health and Sustainability in Sales	194
Law 46: Maintain a High Energy Level	195
Law 47: Avoid Burnout	198
Law 48: Embrace the Journey of Constant Growth!	201
Final Chapter: The Symphony of Sales Success	204
Books By This Author	207
	211

INTRODUCTION

Welcome to "The 48 Laws of Sales," a definitive guide crafted from theoretical selling frameworks and the trenches of actual sales experiences. Whether you are a novice just starting your journey in the vast world of sales or a seasoned professional aiming to refine your skills, this book offers timeless wisdom distilled into 48 essential laws. These laws culminate decades of firsthand experiences, successes, and lessons learned from the front lines of sales across various industries. My purpose in offering this book is to share the principles that have enabled countless professionals to enhance their sales approach, achieving beyond their goals in both their careers and personal lives.

PURPOSE OF THE BOOK

The art of selling is often perceived as a talent one possesses inherently or does not. However, through my years of experience, I have learned that sales is a skill that can be developed and honed with the proper guidance and practice. The purpose of this book is to provide that guidance. Each law in this book serves as a cornerstone for successful sales careers. Mastering these laws will equip you with the tools to effectively communicate the value of your offerings, forge lasting relationships with clients, navigate complex negotiations, and close deals consistently.

Why is mastering these laws crucial for sales success? Because sales is not merely about transactions; it's about connections. It's about understanding the needs and desires of people and finding ways to meet them creatively and effectively. It's about building trust and credibility, without which even the best product or service remains unsold. It's about adapting to ever-changing market conditions and customer preferences. Mastering sales laws is synonymous with learning the art of adaptation, communication, and strategic thinking.

How To Use This Book

This book is designed to serve as both a reference and a workbook. Each law is clearly defined, followed by practical applications, real-life examples, and strategic advice. Here's how you can maximize your benefit from "The 48 Laws of Sales":

1. Read Through Each Law Sequentially: While each law can stand alone, they are placed in a sequence that builds upon each other. Start from the first and move through to the forty-eighth to understand the progression and integration of concepts.

2. Apply as You Go: After reading each law, take a moment to reflect on how it applies to your current sales practices. Are there adjustments you can make immediately? Is there a particular approach that could be refined or enhanced?

3. Take Notes and Set Goals: Use the margins or a notebook to jot down key insights and personal goals. How will you implement a specific law in your daily sales interactions? Setting practical goals will help you translate theory into action.

4. Revisit Frequently: Sales are dynamic; as you grow and the market evolves, different laws will become more relevant at various times. Make this book a frequent reference point to remind yourself of the foundational principles and advanced strategies.

5. Engage with Exercises and Workshops: At the end of each section, exercises and hypothetical scenarios are provided to help you practice the laws in a controlled environment. Engage with these exercises seriously—they are designed to challenge your understanding and improve your sales acumen.

6. Share and Discuss: Sales often thrive collaboratively. Discuss

these laws with your peers, mentors, or team members. Sharing insights and experiences can provide new perspectives and enhance understanding.

7. Reflect on Your Progress: Regularly assess how applying these laws affects your sales results. Reflect on what's working and what needs adjustment. Continuous improvement is a vital theme of this book and should also be a key theme in your career.

Through "The 48 Laws of Sales," you are embarking on a journey to improve your sales techniques and transform your approach to communicating, negotiating, and building relationships. This book isn't just about making better salespeople; it's about better communicators and strategic thinkers—skills invaluable in every aspect of life. Welcome to your next step in mastering the sales process.

PART ONE THE FUNDAMENTALS OF SALES

LAW 1: KNOW YOUR PRODUCT INSIDE OUT

Knowledge is not just power in sales—it is your most crucial asset. This law underpins a fundamental truth: you cannot sell something effectively without understanding it. The importance of product knowledge cannot be overstated. Being an expert in what you're selling transforms your role from a mere vendor to a trusted advisor.

Product Knowledge Is The Backbone Of Effective Selling For Several Reasons

1. It Gives You Confidence in What Selling: Knowing your product inside out instills natural confidence in your sales pitch. This contagious confidence makes it easier to convince potential customers of the value of your product. When you know every feature, benefit, and even product limitation, you speak with authority, which builds trust with your customers.

2. Ability to Handle Objections: Sales rarely go smoothly. Prospects often have objections or concerns that need to be addressed before purchasing. In-depth product knowledge allows you to handle these objections effectively and turn potential deal-breakers into opportunities for further engagement.

3. Customized Solutions: Understanding every aspect of your

product means you can tailor your pitch to meet each customer's specific needs. When you know how your product can solve unique problems, you can present it as the best possible solution, increasing the likelihood of a sale.

4. Up-Selling and Cross-Selling: Comprehensive product knowledge isn't just about knowing one item in isolation; it's about understanding how it fits within a broader range of offerings. This understanding allows you to introduce additional products that complement or enhance the original purchase, thereby increasing the overall value to the customer and boosting your sales figures.

Becoming A Product Expert

To know your product inside out, you must go beyond the basic features and specifications. Here's how you can deepen your product knowledge:

1. Study the Product: Begin with the basics. Learn about the features, benefits, and potential drawbacks of the product. Understand how it's made, where it comes from, and any unique selling propositions it might have.

2. Use the Product Yourself: If possible, use the product personally. Experiencing the product firsthand can give you insights not apparent from product descriptions alone. This experience can provide anecdotal evidence that can be very persuasive during sales conversations.

3. Talk to Product Developers: Engage with those who created the product. This can provide insights into the intentions behind certain features and the problems they aim to solve. Such insider knowledge can be particularly compelling to customers.

4. Gather Customer Feedback: Listen to what customers say about the product. Their praises and their complaints are equally valuable. Understanding their experiences can help you address potential concerns proactively and highlight benefits that resonate most with users.

5. Keep Updated: Stay informed about any updates, changes, or new releases related to your product. The market evolves, and so should your knowledge.

Communicating Your Knowledge

Knowing your product is only half the battle; communicating this knowledge effectively is just as important. Here are some tips to convey your expertise convincingly:

1. Simplify Complex Information: Break down complex information into digestible, relatable terms. Avoid jargon unless you are sure the customer understands it.

2. Focus on Benefits, Not Features: Customers are more interested in how the product can improve their lives rather than its specifications. Link every feature of the product to a

clear, tangible benefit.

3. Prepare for In-Depth Discussions: Be ready to answer deep and technical questions. This preparation shows that you respect the customer's need to make an informed decision.

4. Use Stories and Anecdotes: Share stories of how the product has helped other customers. Personal stories are memorable and can make the product features come alive.

5. Be Honest About Limitations: Honesty about what the product cannot do will enhance your credibility and help manage customer expectations effectively.

Mastering your product knowledge is not merely about memorizing a spec sheet; it's about understanding the product so well that you can make it feel indispensable to your customers. When you know your product inside out, your confidence, expertise, and enthusiasm become infectious, making it significantly easier to close sales and build lasting customer relationships.

LAW 2: UNDERSTAND YOUR CUSTOMER

Every customer is a unique puzzle in sales, and understanding that puzzle is critical to successful selling. The essence of sales lies not in the product sold but in the satisfaction delivered to the customer. Thus, comprehensively understanding who your customers are, what they need, and how they wish to be served is not just beneficial—it's imperative. This law explores the art and science of truly understanding your customer, which is crucial for tailoring your sales approach effectively.

Why Knowing Your Customer Matters

1. Tailored Solutions: The more you know about your customers, the better you can tailor your solutions to their needs. This personalized approach is often the difference between a sale made and a sale missed.

2. Building Relationships: Sales are built on relationships. Understanding your customers allows you to connect personally, creating trust and loyalty crucial for repeat business and referrals.

3. Effective Communication: When you understand your customer's preferences, background, and language, you can communicate more effectively. This alignment in communication reduces misunderstandings and enhances

customer satisfaction.

4. Predicting Needs: By understanding past behaviors and preferences, you can anticipate what your customers might need in the future, positioning you as a proactive problem-solver rather than a reactive salesperson.

Gaining A Deep Understanding Of Your Customers Involves Several Strategies, Each Contributing To A Holistic View Of Who Your Customers Are And What They Value

1. Gather Insights Through Research: Gather insights into your customer base through quantitative and qualitative research methods. Use surveys, customer interviews, and ethnographic studies to uncover your customers' motivations, preferences, and behaviors. These insights can guide your sales strategies and help you connect more effectively.

2. Utilize CRM Systems: Customer Relationship Management (CRM) systems are invaluable in tracking customer interactions, purchases, and feedback. These systems help create detailed customer profiles that can inform your sales approach.

3. Listen Actively: During interactions, listen more than you speak. Pay attention to the customer's words, tone, and body language. Active listening can reveal what they are saying and what they might be hesitant to express directly.

4. Engage on Social Media: Social media platforms are a goldmine of customer data. Engage with customers on these platforms, monitor their comments, and participate in conversations to gain insights into their daily lives and preferences.

5. Follow Trends: Stay updated with industry trends and general consumer behavior changes. Understanding broader trends can help you anticipate shifts in customer desires and expectations.

6. Develop Empathy: Put yourself in your customers' shoes. Understanding their challenges, fears, and aspirations will help you serve them better and forge stronger connections.

Communicating With Your Customers

Knowing your customer is the first step; effectively communicating based on that knowledge is the next. Here are some tips for refining your communication:

1. Customize Your Communication: Tailor your messages based on the customer's profile. This customization might involve adapting your language, tone, or communication channels (email, phone, in-person, social media).

2. Be Relevant and Concise: Ensure your communication is relevant to the customer's needs and interests. Avoid overwhelming them with unnecessary information.

3. Provide Value with Every Interaction: Each interaction should deliver value, whether it's informational, educational, or just making their day more straightforward or more pleasant.

4. Seek Feedback Actively: Encourage and listen to feedback. It's a direct line to understanding your customer's satisfaction and expectations.

5. Maintain Regular Contact: Don't let the relationship lapse. Regular check-ins, updates, and follow-ups keep the relationship warm and demonstrate an ongoing commitment to their satisfaction.

Understanding your customer is not a one-time task but a continuous effort. It requires dedication, attention to detail, and a genuine curiosity about the people you serve. By mastering this law, you equip yourself not just to meet but to exceed the expectations of those you do business with, creating lasting relationships that are both profitable and fulfilling.

LAW 3: BUILD GENUINE RELATIONSHIPS

Relationships are not just meaningful; they are everything. Building and maintaining genuine relationships is a cornerstone of successful selling. It's not merely about making connections to secure a transaction today; it's about forging bonds that yield dividends well into the future. This law emphasizes the importance of relationships in sales and business and outlines strategies for developing these essential connections.

Why Relationships Matter In Sales

1. Trust and Loyalty: Sales based on genuine relationships tend to generate customer trust and loyalty, which are critical for repeat business and long-term success. Customers loyal to a salesperson or a brand are more likely to repurchase and recommend the company to others.

2. Competitive Advantage: In competitive markets, products and prices might be similar. The quality of the relationship with the salesperson or company can often determine a customer's choice.

3. Customer Retention: Retaining an existing customer is generally more cost-effective than acquiring a new one. Strong relationships increase customer retention rates, reducing

overall marketing and sales costs.

4. Higher Value Transactions: Customers who feel a strong relationship and trust with a salesperson are more likely to be receptive to upselling and cross-selling efforts, leading to higher value transactions.

5. Resilience to Problems: When issues arise, as they inevitably do, strong relationships can help mitigate the fallout. A customer who feels genuinely valued is more likely to be understanding and patient while solutions are being sought.

Building Genuine Relationships

Creating and maintaining genuine sales relationships requires effort, sincerity, and strategy. Here are essential practices to help you build these critical connections:

1. Be Authentic: Authenticity forms the foundation of any genuine relationship. Be yourself, and let your personality shine through. People are more likely to trust and relate to someone genuine than someone who seems to be playing a role.

2. Understand Their Needs: Understanding your customer's needs and preferences signifies that you value them. Use this understanding to provide personalized service addressing their circumstances and challenges.

3. Consistent Communication: Keep in touch with your customers regularly, not just when you want to make a sale. Regular communication through newsletters, emails, social media, or even personal notes can keep you on top of your mind without seeming intrusive.

4. Provide Value Beyond Products: Offer your customers value that transcends the products or services you are selling. This could be advice, industry insights, helpful resources, or even introductions to other professionals within your network.

5. Listen More Than You Talk: Good communication is as much about listening as talking. Pay close attention to what your customers say—and what they don't say. Listening actively shows that you care about their opinions and needs.

6. Follow Through on Promises: Trust is built on reliability. Always follow through on your commitments. If you promise to call back with information, do so promptly. Reliability confirms your integrity and the importance you place on the relationship.

7. Celebrate Their Successes: If your customer or their business achieves something noteworthy, celebrate with them. Acknowledging their successes can strengthen your bond, whether a quick congratulatory message or something more substantial.

8. Handle Problems Efficiently: When problems arise, address

them swiftly and efficiently. Proactively solving issues can turn a potentially harmful situation into a positive experience.

9. Seek Feedback: Regularly ask for feedback on your products, services, and overall business experience. This provides valuable insights and shows that you value their opinion and are committed to continuous improvement.

10. Be Patient: Building genuine relationships takes time. Be patient in nurturing these connections. Investing time and effort will pay off in customer loyalty and satisfaction.

The Impact Of Genuine Relationships

The impact of genuine relationships in business extends beyond individual sales. These relationships create a trust, advocacy, and mutual success network that can propel your business forward. They turn customers into champions of your brand, creating a ripple effect that attracts new customers and opens doors to new opportunities. In essence, when you focus on building genuine relationships, you are not just selling a product but building a community around your brand.

By prioritizing genuine relationships, you set the stage for sustained business success, creating a legacy of trust and respect that transcends ordinary transactions and fosters authentic customer engagement.

LAW 4: MASTER THE ART OF LISTENING

Listening is one of the most critical skills in sales, yet it is often the most overlooked. Mastering the art of listening goes beyond merely hearing the spoken words—it involves understanding the complete message being conveyed verbally and non-verbally. This law explores why effective listening is indispensable in sales and how it can transform customer interactions and outcomes.

The Importance Of Listening In Sales

1. Builds Trust and Rapport: When customers feel heard, they develop a sense of trust and rapport with the salesperson. Listening attentively signals respect for their opinions and concerns, fostering trust.

2. Uncovers Customer Needs: Active listening helps you to detect and understand the customer's actual needs, some of which they may not explicitly express. This understanding allows you to tailor your offerings more precisely, which can be the key to closing sales.

3. Reduces Misunderstandings: By paying close attention to what the customer says and clarifying ambiguities, you can significantly reduce misunderstandings and ensure that you provide solutions that meet their expectations.

4. Facilitates Better Responses: Effective listening gives you the insights to formulate more accurate and compelling responses. When you respond in a way that addresses the customer's specific concerns, you demonstrate your commitment to serving their needs.

5. Enhances Customer Satisfaction: Customers who feel listened to are generally more satisfied with the service they receive. This satisfaction can lead to repeat business and positive word-of-mouth, which are invaluable for long-term success.

How To Master The Art Of Listening

Mastering listening in sales involves intentional practices and techniques that go beyond the act of hearing:

1. Focus Fully on the Speaker: Give the speaker your undivided attention. Avoid distractions, refrain from thinking about your response while they are talking, and maintain eye contact to show your engagement.

2. Use Verbal and Non-Verbal Cues: Show that you are listening by nodding, using facial expressions that match the conversation's tone, and employing verbal affirmations like "I see" or "I understand."

3. Reflect and Clarify: Periodically summarize what the customer has said to ensure you have understood them

correctly. Ask clarifying questions to dig deeper into their statements, showing that you are listening and processing the information.

4. Listen for Emotions: Pay attention to the emotions underlying the customer's words. Tone, volume, and pace can give you clues about their emotional state and priorities, which can guide how you respond.

5. Be Patient: Do not interrupt the customer. Allow them to finish their thoughts before you respond. Patience in listening can often reveal more than the initial few sentences might suggest.

6. Take Notes: In situations where details are crucial, notes can help you keep track of key points and follow up effectively. It also signals to the customer that you take their words seriously.

7. Respond Thoughtfully: Once you have fully understood the customer's point of view, craft your responses to address their needs and concerns directly. Tailored responses, based on careful listening, are often the most effective.

The Strategic Value Of Listening

Listening is a strategic tool in sales. It enables you to position yourself as a solution provider rather than just a product seller. By mastering the art of listening, you can:

1. Identify Cross-Selling and Upselling Opportunities: By understanding the broader context of the customer's needs, you can identify additional products or services that could benefit them.

2. Navigate Complex Sales: In complex sales scenarios involving multiple stakeholders and needs, listening becomes crucial in understanding the various perspectives and requirements.

3. Build Long-Term Relationships: Customers are more likely to become long-term clients if they feel that their sales representatives genuinely listen and respond to their needs over time.

4. Differentiate from Competitors: In a marketplace where many salespeople are focused solely on pitching, those who listen effectively can differentiate themselves and create a competitive advantage.

By embracing and refining your listening skills, you improve your immediate sales interactions and build a foundation for business success. Mastering the art of listening transforms you from a transactional seller to a trusted advisor, a transition that can lead to more sales, happier customers, and a more rewarding career in sales.

LAW 5: ALWAYS BE CLOSING

The axiom "Always Be Closing," often abbreviated as ABC, encapsulates a fundamental principle in sales: the objective of every sales interaction is to move towards a close. This law isn't just about persistently asking for the sale; it's about cultivating the mindset and adopting the techniques that consistently lead to sales success. Understanding various closing techniques and recognizing the critical importance of actively pursuing the close can significantly enhance your sales effectiveness.

The Importance Of The Closing Mentality

The close is not merely a final step but a culmination of all preceding efforts. Without the close, all prior rapport-building needs analysis, and solution presentation is without fruit. Embracing a closing mentality means:

1. Being Proactive: Always look for opportunities to guide the customer towards making a decision.

2. Staying Customer-Focused: Tailor every interaction to steer towards solutions that meet the customer's needs.

3. Creating Urgency: Employ strategies that compel the customer to act sooner rather than later.

4. Overcoming Objections: View objections not as roadblocks but as opportunities to refine and reinforce your pitch towards the close.

Different Types Of Closes

Mastering different closing techniques allows you to adapt to various sales scenarios and customer personalities. Here are some of the most effective closing strategies:

1. The Assumptive Close: This technique uses language that assumes the sale has been made. You might say, "When would be the best time to deliver your new car?" instead of asking if they have decided to purchase it. This approach subtly encourages customers to think beyond the decision to utilize the product.

2. The Summary Close: Recap the items or features the customer has shown interest in to remind them of their initial excitement and agreement throughout the conversation. This close helps solidify the value of the purchase and brings the customer back to a positive state of mind about the decision.

3. The Now-or-Never Close: Create a sense of urgency by informing the customer that the opportunity might not be available later. For example, mention a limited-time offer or the last item in stock to encourage immediate action.

4. The Question Close: Instead of telling the customer why they should buy, ask them a question that leads them to talk themselves into the purchase. Questions like, "Do you see how this product can help streamline your workflow?" engage the customer and make them an active participant in the closing process.

5. Option Close: Give the customer choices that lead to a sale. For instance, "Would you prefer the standard or the deluxe version?" This technique reduces the psychological load of a yes/no decision and focuses on finer preferences.

6. The Suggestion Close: Suggest add-ons or supplementary products that complement the primary purchase. This increases the order value and enhances customer satisfaction by providing a complete solution.

7. The Objection Solving Close: Once you've successfully addressed all customer objections, ask for the sale directly, as there should be no further barriers. This could be as straightforward as "It sounds like we've covered everything you need. Shall we go ahead with the order?"

You Can't Close If You Don't Ask

A common pitfall in sales is the reluctance to ask for the sale directly. This hesitation can stem from fear of rejection or the belief that customers will do so without a prompt if they want to buy. However, this approach often leads to missed opportunities. Sales professionals must cultivate the courage to ask for the sale explicitly:

1. Direct Closing: Be direct at the end of your pitch. Ask, "Are you ready to proceed with the purchase?" It's simple and effective.

2. Feedback Loop: Use closing as a feedback mechanism. If the

customer isn't ready to close, their responses can guide you on what additional information or reassurance they need.

The Art Of Persistent Closing

"Always Be Closing" does not mean pushing the customer aggressively. It means consistently aligning the sales process towards the close with tact and skill. It's about making closing a natural part of the conversation, where every question, every feature highlighted, and every objection handled subtly steers towards finalizing the sale.

In mastering the art of closing, you turn potential into actuality. By developing various closing techniques and the confidence to ask directly, you increase your sales effectiveness and enhance the customer experience by providing clear paths to satisfying their needs. This approach ensures that your sales efforts culminate in success, reflecting your understanding of the customer and mastery of the sales process.

Overview Of The Fundamentals Of Sales

In this first section of "The 48 Laws of Sales," we explore the foundational aspects of sales that are critical to your success as a sales professional. These laws cover everything from product knowledge to closing techniques, equipping you with the essential tools to build a solid sales foundation. Engage with the exercises and hypothetical scenarios provided at the end of each law to deepen your understanding and enhance your practical sales skills.

Law 1: Know Your Product Inside Out

Exercise: Create a detailed product fact sheet with comprehensive information beyond the basics.

Hypothetical Scenario: Craft a tailored pitch for a client considering a competitor's cheaper alternative, highlighting your product's unique features.

Law 2: Understand Your Customer

Exercise: Develop a detailed customer persona and tailor a sales approach specifically for this persona.

Hypothetical Scenario: Devise questions and strategies for a potential client currently using a competitor's product, focusing on switching their preference to your product.

Law 3: Build Genuine Relationships

Exercise: Implement relationship-building strategies with existing clients and track the evolution of these relationships over time.

Hypothetical Scenario: Design a client appreciation strategy for a long-term client, looking at competitors' offers and focusing on reinforcing the relationship.

Law 4: Master The Art Of Listening

Exercise: Analyze a recorded sales call to improve the balance of talking versus listening.

Hypothetical Scenario: Script a response to a customer who mentions an unrelated issue during a presentation, showing how your product can indirectly resolve their problem.

Law 5: Always Be Closing

Exercise: Role-play different closing techniques tailored to various customer interactions.

Hypothetical Scenario: Address a client's concerns at the end of a sales meeting, using a suitable closing technique to secure a commitment.

Conclusion

Mastering sales fundamentals involves more than just understanding the basic principles; it's about applying them in real-world scenarios to see tangible improvements in your sales performance. The exercises and scenarios included in this section are designed to challenge you and enhance your sales acumen. They will prepare you to meet and exceed your sales targets by building stronger customer relationships, listening more effectively, and closing deals confidently. As you work through these exercises, reflect on how each law can be integrated into your daily sales practices to transform your approach and results.

PART TWO ADVANCE SALES STRATEGIES

LAW 6: SOLVE PROBLEMS, NOT PUSH PRODUCTS

The distinction between solving problems and merely pushing products can make or break your success. The best salespeople see themselves as problem solvers, not just vendors pushing products. They understand that sales are not just transactions but opportunities to impact their customers' lives and businesses positively. This law delves into the philosophy and strategies behind becoming a problem solver, which leads to higher sales success and builds lasting customer loyalty.

The Philosophy Of Problem-Solving In Sales

Understanding your role as a problem solver involves a shift in mindset from selling products to offering solutions. This approach requires understanding your customers' needs, challenges, and goals. It's about aligning what you deal with and how it can address specific problems or improve the customer's situation.

1. Customer-Centric Approach: Start by listening to your customers to understand their pain points fully. This knowledge allows you to position your product as a solution rather than a mere item for purchase.

2. Building Trust: Customers are more likely to trust your recommendations When they see you are focused on helping

them solve problems. Trust is foundational in converting and retaining loyal customers.

3. Long-Term Relationships: Solving real problems creates value for customers, leading to repeat business, referrals, and enduring relationships.

To Effectively Solve Problems Rather Than Push Products, Employ These Strategies

1. Needs Analysis: Conduct thorough needs analyses through interviews, surveys, and observation. Understand not just what your customers say they want but why they want it and what they are trying to achieve.

2. Educate Your Customers: Often, customers aren't aware of the solutions available to them. Education can involve blogs, webinars, demonstrations, or detailed discussions about how specific features of your product can resolve their issues.

3. Customize Solutions: Tailor your offerings to meet the customer's specific needs. This might involve customizing products, creating bundles, or offering scalable solutions that grow with the customer's needs.

4. Consultative Selling: Adopt a consultative approach, where you act more like an advisor than a traditional salesperson. This approach emphasizes guidance and tailored advice, building a partnership rather than a vendor-client relationship.

5. Feedback and Adaptation: After offering a solution, follow up to see how it's working and adapt as necessary. Continuous improvement based on customer feedback shows commitment to genuinely solving problems.

6. Solution-Based Pitching: When presenting your product, focus your pitch on how the features specifically address the pain points your customer has expressed. This targeted approach makes the benefits more tangible and relevant.

Real-World Application

Consider a scenario where a business struggles with inefficient inventory management, leading to operational delays and increased costs. Instead of simply selling them the latest inventory management software, a problem-solving salesperson would:

Analyze the specific challenges within the customer's existing processes.

Demonstrate how specific features of the software can streamline operations.

Customize the software setup to meet the customer's logistical and operational needs.

Train staff to maximize the use of new tools.

Follow up to adjust and optimize the software's use as the business evolves.

This approach helps close the sale and ensures the solution improves the customer's business operations, leading to higher satisfaction and loyalty.

Conclusion

Adopting the mindset of a problem solver rather than a product pusher transforms the sales process into a collaborative journey with the customer. It's about creating value beyond the product, fostering relationships built on trust, and establishing yourself as a vital customer resource. By focusing on solving problems, you position yourself and your product as essential to your customer's success, which is the ultimate goal of every outstanding salesperson.

LAW 7: ADAPT TO CUSTOMER NEEDS

"Be like water... Now, you put water into a cup; it becomes the cup; you put water into a bottle, it becomes the bottle; you put it in a teapot, and it becomes the teapot. Now water can flow, or it can crash." – Bruce Lee

This iconic statement by Bruce Lee is not just a martial arts philosophy but a powerful metaphor for sales professionals. The essence of adaptability is crucial in the ever-changing landscape of customer needs and market dynamics. This law explores the importance of adaptability in sales and how it can significantly enhance customer interactions and, ultimately, lead to tremendous sales success.

Understanding Adaptability In Sales

Adaptability in sales means adjusting your approach based on your customers' evolving needs, behaviors, and feedback. It involves being responsive to the market, flexible strategies, and innovative solutions. Being adaptable ensures that you are not just responding to changes but also anticipating them.

1. Customer-Centric Selling: At its core, adaptability is about putting the customer first. It's about understanding that each customer is unique and may require a different approach or solution.

2. Listening Actively: Being adaptable starts with listening. You can understand their explicit needs and implied expectations by genuinely listening to what your customers are saying.

3. Flexibility in Problem-Solving: Adaptability requires flexibility not just in how you respond to problems but also in how you anticipate and prevent them.

Strategies To Enhance Adaptability

To embody the fluidity that Bruce Lee describes and to truly "become the teapot," as he suggests, you need to develop specific strategies to mold your sales techniques to fit any customer scenario.

1. Learn Continuously: The market and customer preferences are constantly changing. Stay informed about industry trends, new tools, and technologies to help you meet customer needs more effectively.

2. Develop a Broad Product Knowledge: Understand not just your product but also how it compares to others in the market. This broad knowledge allows you to adjust your pitch or recommend different solutions based on the customer's values.

3. Customize Communication Styles: Adapt your communication style to match the personality and preferences of each customer. Some may prefer detailed presentations;

others might appreciate concise, bullet-point discussions.

4. Use Feedback to Pivot: Regularly collect and analyze customer feedback to adjust your strategies. This could mean changing a product feature, altering your sales approach, or even modifying after-sales support.

5. Be Proactive, Not Reactive: Anticipate changes in customer needs and market conditions. Develop the ability to foresee and adapt to changes before they become challenges.

Real-World Application: The Adaptive Sales Cycle

Consider the sales cycle as a dynamic journey rather than a static process. Each stage of this cycle can benefit from adaptability:

Prospecting: Tailor your prospecting methods based on the target demographic. Younger audiences might respond better to social media outreach, whereas traditional businesses might appreciate a more formal approach.

Needs Assessment: Use adaptive questioning techniques to uncover current and future needs.

Proposal: Customize proposals to address each customer's business conditions and challenges.

Closure: Be flexible in negotiation. Sometimes, adapting your terms to suit the customer's budget or timeline can secure a sale.

Follow-Up: Adapt your follow-up based on customer feedback from the initial sale. Each follow-up is an opportunity to adjust and improve the customer experience.

Conclusion

Being adaptable in sales, like water in Bruce Lee's philosophy, means you are prepared to transform and flow into whatever shape the situation requires. It is about being versatile, responsive, and resilient—qualities that define good and great salespeople. By cultivating adaptability, you ensure that you can meet your customers wherever they are, with exactly what they need, exactly when they need it. This approach does not just satisfy customers; it delights them, fostering loyalty and driving repeat business.

LAW 8: FOCUS ON QUALITY, NOT JUST QUANTITY

In the competitive sales world, the pressure to meet quotas and drive numbers can often overshadow the fundamental goal of delivering quality. However, top sales professionals understand that long-term success is built on the foundation of quality—not just in the products or services offered but in every interaction with customers. This law underscores why prioritizing quality over quantity is crucial in sales and how it can significantly elevate your reputation, customer satisfaction, and sales results.

The Importance Of Quality In Sales

Quality in sales refers to the value and effectiveness of your interactions, solutions, and overall customer experience. Here are several reasons why focusing on quality is vital:

1. Sustainable Business Growth: Quality leads to customer satisfaction, repeat business, and referrals, which are all sustainable growth drivers. Unlike one-time sales, quality interactions encourage ongoing business relationships.

2. Enhanced Customer Loyalty: Customers return to businesses where they feel valued and satisfied. High-quality interactions and solutions increase customer loyalty, reducing churn and building a stable customer base.

3. Differentiation in Competitive Markets: In markets where customers can choose from many providers, quality can distinguish your offerings from competitors. It's not just about what you sell but how and the service you provide afterward.

4. Higher Profit Margins: While focusing on quantity often leads to competing prices, focusing on quality allows for premium pricing. Customers are willing to pay more for products and services they perceive as high quality.

5. Brand Reputation: Consistent customer interaction quality and product offerings enhance your brand's reputation. A strong reputation attracts more customers and better partnerships and business opportunities.

Strategies To Enhance Quality In Sales

Enhancing quality in sales involves strategic actions and a commitment to excellence. Here are effective strategies to ensure quality in every aspect of the sales process:

1. Invest in Training: Ensure your sales team is well-trained in your products and services, customer service, and communication skills. Continuous training helps maintain a high standard of quality in customer interactions.

2. Implement Robust Processes: Develop and maintain processes that ensure quality checks at every sales cycle stage, from lead

generation to post-sale follow-up. This could include quality assurance teams or feedback mechanisms that monitor and provide high standards.

3. Leverage Technology: Utilize CRM systems and data analytics to track customer interactions and preferences. Technology can help maintain personalization and service quality even as your customer base grows.

4. Encourage Feedback and Adaptation: Regularly seek customer feedback and be willing to adapt your approach or offerings based on that feedback. This openness improves quality and shows customers that you value their input.

5. Prioritize Ethical Selling: Maintain high ethical standards in your sales practices. This includes being honest about your product's capabilities, avoiding overselling, and always acting in the customer's best interest.

Conclusion

Focusing on quality over quantity in sales is about improving current transactions and building a sustainable business that thrives on customer loyalty, robust partnerships, and a strong market reputation. By prioritizing quality, you align your business practices with your customers' long-term values and needs, leading to deeper relationships and consistent sales success. This approach guarantees survival and success in today's competitive business environment.

LAW 9: DEVELOP A CONSISTENT SALES PROCESS

A consistent sales process is pivotal for your success in sales. This structured approach ensures systematic customer engagement and enhances your ability to scale your efforts and improve results over time. In this law, we explore how to establish a sales process that is effective, adaptable, and integral to achieving sales excellence.

Implementing A Consistent Sales Process Offers Several Key Benefits That Can Transform Your Sales Efforts

1. Predictability: Knowing what to do at each step of the sales journey helps you anticipate outcomes, manage your pipeline more effectively, and fine-tune your strategies based on what works.

2. Efficiency: A streamlined process reduces time spent per sale and minimizes potential errors or redundant efforts, allowing you to handle more customers or close deals faster.

3. Enhanced Training: With a straightforward process, you can onboard new roles or adopt new strategies more quickly and effectively.

4. Uniform Customer Experience: Ensuring every customer interaction is consistent improves their overall experience, boosting satisfaction and loyalty.

5. Performance Measurement: Standardizing your sales approach makes it easier to measure your success and identify areas for improvement.

Core Elements Of Your Sales Process

While your specific sales process may vary depending on your industry or product, specific foundational steps are universally beneficial:

1. Lead Generation: Develop strategies to identify and attract potential customers. This might include online marketing, networking, or partnerships.

2. Lead Qualification: Assess which leads have the potential to purchase based on factors like their need, budget, and decision-making power.

3. Needs Analysis: Deeply understand the challenges and requirements of your potential customers to tailor your solutions effectively.

4. Proposal: Craft compelling proposals that clearly articulate

the benefits of your solutions, tailored to each customer's specific needs.

5. Handling Objections: Equip yourself with the knowledge and skills to address customer concerns and remove sales barriers.

6. Closing: Employ effective closing techniques to finalize the deal, ensuring the customer is committed and satisfied.

7. Follow-Up: Maintain the relationship after the sale to support and engage your customers, fostering repeat business and referrals.

Implementing And Refining Your Sales Process

Here's how you can develop and maintain an effective sales process:

1. Document Each Step: Clearly define what needs to happen at each stage. This helps you stay on track and is a valuable tool for continuous improvement.

2. Align with the Customer Journey: Make sure your sales process matches your customers' purchasing decisions. Understanding their journey from awareness to decision can help you adjust to serve them better.

3. Leverage Technology: Use tools like CRM systems to manage customer interactions, automate tasks, and track progress through your sales funnel.

4. Continuous Training: Regularly update your skills and knowledge to reflect changes in your sales process and the broader market.

5. Measure and Optimize: Use performance metrics to assess the effectiveness of each stage of your sales process. Look for trends and patterns that indicate success or opportunities for improvement.

Conclusion

Developing a consistent sales process is not just about establishing a routine; it's about creating a reliable and practical framework that supports all your sales activities. Understanding and implementing each step of this process ensures that every customer interaction moves smoothly toward a successful closure. This approach doesn't just make your job easier; it enhances the entire experience for your customers, leading to better outcomes and higher satisfaction on both sides.

LAW 10: BE PASSIONATE ABOUT WHAT YOU SELL

Passion is a powerful force in any profession, but it's a critical element that can differentiate a good salesperson from a great one. This law explores the transformative impact of passion on your sales efforts, how it influences customer perceptions, and, ultimately, how it drives sales success.

The Power Of Passion In Sales

Being passionate about what you sell does more than energize your daily activities—it resonates with customers, builds trust, and establishes long-term relationships. Here's why passion is so crucial:

1. Enhances Credibility: Your genuine enthusiasm and belief in your products or services enhances your credibility. Customers are more likely to trust your recommendations when they see that you are sincerely convinced of the benefits of your selling.

2. Increases Engagement: Passion is contagious. Your enthusiasm can catch customers' interest and attention more effectively than any sales script. When you are excited about your offering, it naturally piques the curiosity of your customers, encouraging them to learn more.

3. Drives Persistence: Sales can be challenging, with many ups and downs. Passion for what you do fuels your drive to persist through rejections and setbacks. This resilience is essential for long-term success in sales.

4. Fosters Connection and Empathy: Being passionate lets you connect with customers more deeply. It helps you communicate not just the features of your product but also its impact and value in a way that resonates emotionally with customers.

5. Supports Value-Based Selling: Passion shifts your selling approach from transactional to value-based. You're not just selling a product; you're offering a solution you genuinely believe can make a difference in the customer's life or business.

Cultivating And Communicating Passion

While some might naturally feel passionate about their products or services, passion can also be cultivated and nurtured through various practices:

1. Believe in Your Product: To develop genuine passion, believe in what you're selling. Understand the benefits and impact of your product thoroughly. Use your product personally and gather success stories from satisfied customers.

2. Connect With Your Why: Understanding why you're in your specific field can help maintain your passion. Knowing your '

why ' can keep your love alive, whether it's a personal connection to the product or an alignment with the company's mission.

3. Stay Informed and Inspired: Keep up-to-date with industry trends, product advancements, and success stories. Continuous learning not only keeps you informed but also inspired.

4. Share Your Successes and Challenges: Sharing your experiences with colleagues and mentors can reinforce your passion. Discussing successes and challenges keeps your emotional connection to your work vibrant and real.

5. Practice Authenticity: Let your true self shine through in your sales interactions. Authenticity strengthens the trust customers have in you and can make your passion more palpable and relatable.

Conclusion

Being passionate about what you sell transforms your approach to sales from performing a duty to sharing a conviction. This transformation enhances satisfaction and success rates and profoundly influences how customers perceive and interact with you. Passionate salespeople are seen as vendors, credible advisors, and partners in their customers' success. By cultivating and communicating your passion, you ensure your sales process is more enjoyable and effective, leading to higher conversion rates, customer satisfaction, and loyalty. Remember, passion isn't just a trait in sales—it's a strategy.

OVERVIEW OF ADVANCED SALES STRATEGIES

In this section of "The 48 Laws of Sales," we investigate the strategies that can elevate your sales approach from basic to advanced. These strategies are designed to refine your techniques, enhance interactions, and drive higher success rates. Practical exercises and hypothetical scenarios accompany each law to help you master these advanced strategies.

Law 6: Solve Problems, Not Push Products

Exercise: Identify a common customer problem and develop a comprehensive solution using your product or service. Document the problem-solving process in a case study format.

Hypothetical Scenario: Imagine a client is considering a cheaper alternative to your product. Outline a conversation where you demonstrate the superior value of your solution by focusing on how it specifically addresses their pain points and long-term needs.

Law 7: Adapt to Customer Needs

Exercise: Conduct a role-playing session where you adapt your sales pitch to suit different customer profiles based on their unique business environments, challenges, and industries.

Hypothetical Scenario: A long-time customer's business model has evolved and needs a more scalable solution. Prepare a tailored upgrade proposal demonstrating your understanding of their new requirements and how your solutions can develop alongside their business.

Law 8: Focus on Quality, Not Just Quantity

Exercise: Review your current sales targets and strategies. Propose adjustments to focus more on high-quality leads rather than high quantities of leads. Develop criteria for identifying and prioritizing these high-quality prospects.

Hypothetical Scenario: You notice a decline in customer retention rates. Create a plan to improve satisfaction and loyalty and enhance the quality of follow-ups and customer engagement.

Law 9: Develop a Consistent Sales Process

Exercise: Map out your existing sales process and identify areas where inconsistencies occur. Implement standard operating procedures (SOPs) for each stage of the sales process to ensure uniformity and effectiveness.

Hypothetical Scenario: A new product is being launched, and you need to integrate it into your existing sales process. Sketch out how you would introduce this product to different segments of your customer base using your standardized sales steps.

Law 10: Be Passionate About What You Sell

Exercise: Write a personal mission statement that connects your values and passions with your product or service's benefits. Reflect on this statement before each customer interaction to align your passion with your sales approach.

Hypothetical Scenario: During a sales slump, your motivation wanes. Develop a presentation or a sales pitch that rekindles your enthusiasm for your product by focusing on its impact on customers' lives or businesses.

Conclusion

Mastering advanced sales strategies requires a deep understanding of the techniques and philosophy behind each approach. The exercises and scenarios in this section are designed to challenge your thinking, sharpen your skills, and ensure you are equipped to handle complex sales situations with expertise and confidence. Applying these laws will improve your sales outcomes and enhance the overall quality of your interactions, leading to a more fulfilling and successful sales experience.

PART THREE: BUILDING TRUST AND TRANSPARENCY

LAW 11: BE TRANSPARENT WITH CLIENTS

In sales, transparency isn't just a good practice—it's essential for building lasting relationships and maintaining a positive reputation. This law focuses on the importance of being transparent with your clients, detailing how such openness influences trust, client satisfaction, and, ultimately, the success of your business.

Transparency Is Crucial In Sales For Several Reasons:

1. Trust Building: Clients trust transparent sellers more readily. When you are clear about your product's capabilities and limitations, clients are more likely to believe in your integrity and have confidence in your advice.

2. Prevents misunderstandings: Clear and open communication ensures that both parties have the same understanding, reducing the likelihood of conflicts arising from misunderstandings.

3. Fosters Loyalty: Customers who feel they are being treated honestly are likelier to remain loyal to your brand. Loyalty not only leads to repeat business but also enhances word-of-mouth marketing.

4. Strengthens Your Brand: A reputation for transparency can significantly bolster your brand's image. In a market where consumers are bombarded with choices, being known for honest practices can be a crucial differentiator.

5. Encourages Engagement: When clients know that a salesperson is transparent, they are more likely to engage openly, provide feedback, and communicate their needs effectively.

To Practice Transparency Effectively, Consider The Following Approaches

1. Clear Communication: Use simple, direct language that clients can easily understand. Avoid technical jargon or vague terms that might confuse or mislead.

2. Full Disclosure: Always disclose all relevant information about pricing, product capabilities, and potential drawbacks. Ensure the client understands what they agree on regarding product offerings and service conditions.

3. Honest Promotions: Market your product honestly. Highlight its strengths without exaggerating its benefits or capabilities. Be upfront about any limitations to set realistic expectations.

4. Acknowledge Mistakes: If an error occurs, acknowledge it immediately and take steps to rectify it. Clients respect and trust

professionals who can admit mistakes and are committed to making things right.

5. Accessibility of Information: Provide easy access to detailed product information, terms of service, and customer testimonials. Ensure that all promotional materials are accurate and up-to-date.

Conclusion

Embracing transparency in your sales interactions is fundamental to establishing a trustworthy relationship with your clients. Being open and honest at every stage of the sales process enhances customer satisfaction and loyalty and builds a robust and reputable brand that stands out in the marketplace. Transparency is not just about adhering to ethical practices; it's a strategic approach that drives real business success by aligning your goals with the needs and expectations of your clients. Remember, when you are transparent, you empower your clients to make informed decisions, which is the cornerstone of any successful business relationship.

LAW 12: BE HONEST IN ALL DEALINGS

Honesty is the cornerstone of any successful business relationship. In the sales world, being honest with your clients isn't just a moral obligation—it's a strategic imperative that can distinguish you from competitors and build lasting loyalty. This law discusses the importance of honesty in all dealings, how it benefits both the seller and the client, and practical ways to integrate it into every interaction.

Honesty Is Essential For Several Key Reasons:

1. Builds Trust: Trust is the foundation of any relationship, especially in sales. Honesty establishes you as a trustworthy and reliable partner, encouraging clients to feel secure in business decisions.

2. Enhances Reputation: Your reputation as a salesperson or a business is built over time through consistent, honest interactions. A reputation for integrity can become one of your most valuable assets, attracting new customers and retaining existing ones.

3. Reduces Risk of Backlash: Dishonesty can lead to customer dissatisfaction, complaints, and negative reviews, significantly damaging your brand and sales. Being honest helps avoid these risks by setting realistic expectations from the start.

4. Encourages Repeat Business: Customers are more likely to return to a business they trust. Honesty in sales fosters loyalty, which is crucial for long-term success and growth.

5. Fosters a Positive Work Environment: A culture of honesty in a business impacts external relationships with customers and internal dynamics among team members. It encourages a positive, ethical working environment.

Incorporating Honesty Into Your Sales Process Involves Several Actionable Steps:

1. Transparent Communication: Communicate product details, pricing, and policies. Avoid hiding fees or conditions in the fine print. Be upfront about what your product can and cannot do.

2. Set Realistic Expectations: Manage expectations by being realistic about outcomes and timelines. It's better to under-promise and over-deliver than to make promises you can't keep.

3. Handle Mistakes Openly: If a mistake happens, whether a delayed shipment or a billing error, address it promptly and transparently. Apologize and offer a solution or compensation to demonstrate your commitment to fairness.

4. Avoid Misleading Tactics: Steer clear of deceptive sales tactics. This includes exaggerating benefits, providing misleading information, or omitting critical product limitations.

Conclusion

Being honest in all your dealings solidifies your integrity and trustworthiness in the eyes of your clients. It's about more than just avoiding deceit—it's about actively cultivating transparency, reliability, and respect in every interaction. This approach ensures compliance with ethical standards and significantly enhances customer satisfaction and loyalty. Ultimately, honesty in sales is not just good practice; it's good business. Committing to honesty builds a reputable brand that customers are proud to associate with and recommend to others.

LAW 13: FOCUS ON BUILDING TRUST

Trust is fundamental in any relationship, but it's especially paramount in sales. Trust influences how customers perceive your brand, decide on purchases, and engage with your company long-term. This law examines the critical importance of building trust, outlines the benefits of trust-based relationships, and provides practical steps to foster trust with your clients.

Trust Acts As The Backbone Of Successful Sales Interactions For Several Compelling Reasons:

1. Facilitates Open Communication: When customers trust you, they're more likely to communicate openly about their needs, concerns, and expectations. This open dialogue is essential for effective sales and customer satisfaction.

2. Enhances Customer Loyalty: Trust leads to customer loyalty, as customers prefer to do business with people and companies they trust. Loyal customers are also more likely to provide repeat business and referrals.

3. Reduces Purchase Anxiety: Many customers experience anxiety when making significant purchases. Trust in a salesperson can alleviate these fears, making the purchasing process smoother and more enjoyable.

4. Supports Premium Pricing: Customers are willing to pay a premium for products and services when they trust the quality and reliability of what they're buying and whom they're buying from.

5. Strengthens Your Brand's Reputation: A trustworthy reputation is invaluable. It can protect and elevate your brand above competitors, especially in industries where trust is critical to customer decision-making.

Strategies For Building Trust

Building trust doesn't happen overnight, but with consistent effort and genuine interaction, you can establish and maintain trust effectively:

1. Consistency in Words and Actions: Ensure that your actions consistently match your words. Reliability in keeping promises and fulfilling commitments is vital to building trust.

2. Transparency: Be transparent in all your dealings. This includes being clear about product capabilities, pricing, and policies and being honest about potential drawbacks.

3. Expertise and Knowledge: Demonstrate deep knowledge of your products and the industry. Customers trust salespeople who can competently answer their questions and provide valuable insights.

4. Personal Integrity: Uphold high ethical standards in all your interactions. Avoid deceptive practices and always act in the best interest of your customers.

5. Empathy and Understanding: Show genuine care for your customers' needs and problems. Empathy can create a solid emotional connection, further solidifying trust.

6. Proactive Problem Solving: Address issues before they become problems for your customers. Being proactive not only shows that you care but also that you are dependable.

7. Follow-Up: Follow up with your customers after a sale to ensure they are satisfied. This improves customer experience and reinforces their decision to trust you.

Conclusion

Focusing on building trust is crucial for long-term success in sales. Trust influences nearly every aspect of the customer journey, from initial contact through post-sale support. By prioritizing trust-building in your sales strategy, you create more than just transactions; you develop enduring relationships that benefit your customers and your business. Trust leads to deeper loyalty, more significant engagement, and sustained business growth. Remember, when trust goes up, speed also

LAW 14: MAINTAIN PROFESSIONAL INTEGRITY

Professional integrity in sales is not just about adhering to ethical guidelines—it's about embodying values that foster trust, respect, and long-term success. This law discusses the crucial role of integrity in building a sustainable career in sales, its impact on relationships with clients and colleagues, and how it influences your personal and professional reputation.

The Importance Of Integrity In Sales

Integrity is a cornerstone of professional success in any field. Still, in sales, its importance is magnified due to the direct interaction with customers and the impact of those interactions on business outcomes.

1. Cultivates Trust: Integrity builds deep trust between you and your clients. When clients know they can rely on you, to be honest and forthright, they are likelier to do business with you repeatedly and refer others to you.

2. Enhances Credibility: Your credibility is your currency in sales. Maintaining integrity ensures that your word is valued and trusted, which is critical in negotiations and when closing deals.

3. Supports Long-Term Success: While deceptive practices might offer short-term gains, integrity lays the foundation for long-term success and sustainability in your sales career. It helps you build lasting relationships based on respect and mutual benefit.

4. Protects Your Reputation: In the digital age, where information is readily accessible, your reputation can be your greatest asset or most significant liability. Integrity protects and enhances your reputation, making attracting new clients and opportunities easier.

5. Reduces Legal and Ethical Risks: Adhering to high ethical standards minimizes the risk of legal issues and penalties related to deceptive sales practices. It ensures compliance with both industry regulations and broader societal ethical standards.

How To Maintain Professional Integrity

Maintaining integrity involves more than just avoiding wrongdoing; it's about proactively fostering ethical behavior in all aspects of your work.

1. Be Honest in All Communications: Always speak truthfully with clients, even when the truth may not be what they want to hear. Transparency about product capabilities, pricing, and the realistic outcomes they can expect is essential.

2. Keep Your Promises: Fulfill all commitments you make to clients and colleagues. If circumstances change, making it impossible to keep a promise, communicate the situation honestly and promptly.

3. Respect Confidentiality: Handle all client information with the utmost respect and confidentiality. Trust is easily broken and hard to repair if sensitive information is mishandled.

4. Avoid Conflicts of Interest: Avoid situations where your interests might conflict with your clients or employer. If such conflicts arise, disclose them immediately to the relevant parties.

5. Treat Everyone with Respect: Integrity involves respect for everyone, regardless of their status or relationship with you. This respect should extend to clients, colleagues, and competitors alike.

Conclusion

Maintaining professional integrity is fundamental to achieving success and fulfillment in your sales career. It allows you to build meaningful relationships based on trust and respect, navigate challenges confidently, and create a positive impact through your work. By committing to high ethical standards, you set a course for personal growth and professional excellence, ensuring your career is profitable and praiseworthy.

LAW 15: HANDLE OBJECTIONS PROFESSIONALLY

Handling objections is an inevitable part of the sales process. Every salesperson must be prepared to face and address potential customers' concerns or questions about a product or service. This law emphasizes the importance of managing these objections professionally, offering strategies to turn potential deal-breakers into opportunities for enhancing customer understanding and trust.

Objection Handling Is Crucial For Several Reasons:

1. **Builds Credibility:** Effectively addressing objections demonstrates your expertise and confidence in your product or service, which enhances your credibility.

2. Increases Sales Conversion Rates: You clear the path to closing the sale by overcoming objections. Each resolved objection brings the customer closer to making a purchase decision.

3. Improves Product Understanding: Addressing objections often involves providing more detailed information about the product, which can help the customer understand its value more clearly.

4. Strengthens Customer Relationships: Handling objections

carefully and professionally shows that you respect the customer's concerns. This respect can strengthen the relationship, regardless of whether the sale is made.

5. Provides Valuable Feedback: Objections give insight into what potential customers think about your product and what might be lacking. This feedback can be invaluable for adjusting your product or sales approach.

Strategies For Handling Objections Professionally

Effective objection handling requires preparation, understanding, and a strategic approach:

1. Anticipate Common Objections: Prepare for common objections by thoroughly understanding your product and market. Have ready responses that are thoughtful and well-articulated.

2. Listen Actively: Listen carefully without interrupting when a customer objects. Understand the root of their concern—it might not be immediately apparent.

3. Acknowledge and Empathize: Always acknowledge the customer's concerns. Show empathy and validate their feelings to establish a connection and demonstrate that you take their concerns seriously.

4. Respond Clearly and Directly: Address the objection directly with a clear, concise response. Use facts, figures, and specific examples to support your points.

5. Confirm Resolution: Ask the customer if they feel their concern has been resolved after addressing an objection. This ensures that you have dealt with the objection effectively and that the customer feels heard and satisfied.

6. Use Objections to Your Advantage: Turn objections into opportunities to elucidate your product's benefits further. Each objection is a chance to discuss features of your product that may not have been initially apparent.

7. Practice and Refine: Regularly review and practice your responses to objections. Seek feedback from peers or mentors and refine your approach based on real-world experiences.

Conclusion

Handling objections professionally is about defending your product or service and enhancing understanding and trust between you and your customers. By effectively managing objections, you increase your chances of making a sale and build stronger, more trusting relationships. This approach demonstrates that you value the customer's input and are committed to helping them make informed decisions. This commitment fosters a positive reputation for you as a salesperson and your brand, paving the way for future opportunities and success in your sales career.

OVERVIEW OF BUILDING TRUST AND TRANSPARENCY

Part Three of "The 48 Laws of Sales" is dedicated to the pivotal roles of trust and transparency in forging strong and enduring relationships with clients. This section underscores the necessity of building a foundation based on honesty and integrity, which is crucial for sustainable success in sales. Each law discussed here provides actionable strategies to enhance trustworthiness and ensure transparent dealings, accompanied by practical exercises and realistic scenarios that help you master these essential skills.

Law 11: Be Transparent With Clients

Exercise: Audit all client-facing communications for transparency, focusing on clarity and completeness.

Scenario: A client has experienced misleading sales tactics. Plan how to present your product's pricing and terms to rebuild their trust in sales processes.

Law 12: Be Honest In All Dealings

Exercise: Role-play scenarios where you must communicate product limitations honestly, focusing on maintaining client trust.

Scenario: A customer inquires about a feature your product lacks. Script how you would address this honestly while highlighting other valuable features.

Law 13: Focus On Building Trust

Exercise: Regularly check in with existing clients without pushing new sales to build long-term trust.

Scenario: Address a service failure that has shaken a client's trust. Create a plan to restore their confidence through proactive and sincere communication.

Law 14: Maintain Professional Integrity

Exercise: Reflect on recent sales interactions to identify moments when your integrity was challenged, and think about how you responded.

Scenario: You discover a mistake in a proposal that would unfairly benefit your company at the expense of the client. Outline steps to correct this error transparently.

Law 15: Handle Objections Professionally

Exercise: Create a guide for responding to common objections, which can be used to train new sales team members.

Scenario: A prospective client is concerned about your solution's cost and long-term effectiveness. Prepare a detailed response that respects their concerns and clarifies the value.

Conclusion Of Part Three Building Trust And Transparency

The exercises and scenarios in Part Three are designed to deepen your understanding and application of trust and transparency in sales. By engaging in these activities, you refine your ability to communicate openly, address concerns effectively, and maintain ethical standards, which are critical for building lasting relationships with clients. This part of the book ensures you are equipped with the necessary tools to not only meet but exceed customer expectations through principle.

PART FOUR: COMMUNICATION AND PERSUASION

LAW 16: TAILOR YOUR SALES PITCH

Tailoring your sales pitch to suit your potential customers' diverse preferences and decision-making styles is crucial for sales success. This law explores how to customize your approach to various buyer types, enhancing the effectiveness of your pitches and increasing your chances of closing deals.

Importance Of Tailoring Your Sales Pitch

Customizing your pitch ensures you connect more effectively with potential buyers by addressing their needs and buying behaviors. This strategy enhances relevance, builds rapport, increases satisfaction, and improves conversion rates and sales cycle efficiency.

Detailed Buyer Types And Tailoring Strategies

1. The Analytical Buyer

Characteristics: Analytical buyers focus on data, logic, and details. They make decisions based on a thorough evaluation of facts and figures and a clear understanding of the product's benefits and drawbacks.

Tailoring Strategy: Provide detailed product data, back claims with research, including technical specifications, and use logical arguments that highlight product efficiency and utility. Present case studies or white papers that demonstrate your product's effectiveness.

2. The Relational Buyer:

Characteristics: These buyers prioritize relationships and trust. They prefer to buy from salespeople who understand their needs and whom they can view as advisors rather than just vendors.

Tailoring Strategy: Build rapport by engaging in meaningful conversations beyond the transaction. Highlight testimonials and case studies of satisfied customers and emphasize excellent customer service and ongoing support.

3. The Bottom-Line Buyer:

Characteristics: This buyer type is primarily concerned with the cost-effectiveness and efficiency of the product. They are results-oriented and want to quickly understand how your product or service will impact their bottom line.

Tailoring Strategy: Clearly articulate the ROI of your product, use competitive pricing data, and focus on the product's benefits that directly affect profitability and operational efficiency. Keep your pitch concise and focused on financial benefits.

4. The Impulsive Buyer:

Characteristics: Impulsive buyers make quick purchase decisions based on emotional responses. They are often driven by how the product makes them feel or how it fits into their lifestyle.

Tailoring Strategy: Use vivid imagery and emotional appeals in your pitch. Highlight immediate benefits, use storytelling to create a connection, and make the purchase process simple and fast. Limited-time offers and exclusivity can be very effective with this group.

Conclusion

Understanding these buyer types and adapting your sales approach can significantly enhance your ability to connect with and convert potential customers. Each type requires a different strategy that respects their unique preferences and decision-making processes. Recognizing these differences and customizing your pitches will increase sales effectiveness and build stronger, more enduring relationships with your clients.

LAW 17: USE STORYTELLING TO ENGAGE

Storytelling is a powerful tool in sales, transforming standard interactions into memorable experiences. By weaving narratives around your products or services, you can capture the imagination of your audience, making the benefits more tangible and emotionally resonant. This law explores the strategic use of storytelling in sales, detailing how it can enhance engagement, simplify complex information, and create a lasting impact.

Incorporating Storytelling Into Your Sales Approach Offers Several Significant Advantages:

1. Enhances Engagement: Stories capture attention in ways that lists of features or benefits cannot. A good story keeps the listener engaged, making your pitch more memorable.

2. Builds Emotional Connections: Stories often strike emotional chords. Emotions play a crucial role in decision-making, especially in sales. Connecting emotionally can influence how customers feel about your products, which frequently translates into their thoughts.

3. Simplifies Complex Information: Technical products or complex services can be challenging to explain. Stories can help simplify these concepts and make them accessible and relatable

to your audience.

4. Increases Persuasiveness: Stories can illustrate the value of a product or service in a real-world context, making the benefits vivid and concrete rather than abstract and theoretical.

5. Fosters Trust and Credibility: Sharing stories of real people and results can enhance your credibility and make your business more relatable.

Implementing Storytelling In Sales

To effectively use storytelling in your sales strategy, consider the following approaches:

1. Craft Relatable Characters: Develop characters in your stories to which your audience can relate. The character's challenges should mirror the challenges faced by your prospects.

2. Use a Structured Narrative: Every good story has a clear beginning, middle, and end. Start with a relatable problem or pain point, proceed to the intervention (your product/service), and conclude with a successful resolution.

3. Incorporate Customer Testimonials: Real-life success stories and testimonials can be framed as stories. They are particularly effective because they feature actual clients and tangible results.

4. Highlight Before and After Scenarios: Show your prospects what life looks like before and after your product or service. This classic storytelling technique can effectively demonstrate your value proposition.

5. Emphasize Emotional Payoffs: Focus on the emotional rewards of using your product or service. Whether it's peace of mind, joy, or relief, highlighting these emotions can be pivotal in influencing buying decisions.

6. Practice Storytelling: Like any skill, storytelling improves with practice. Rehearse your stories to make sure they are compelling and to the point, ensuring that each one supports the core message of your pitch.

Conclusion

Utilizing storytelling in your sales presentations engages your audience and deeply enhances how your product or service is perceived. Stories can transform abstract concepts into experiences, making them feel real, achievable, and desirable. By mastering the art of storytelling, you make your pitches more effective and build stronger, more emotional connections with your clients, leading to higher engagement, satisfaction, and, ultimately, sales success.

LAW 18: CREATE A SENSE OF URGENCY

Creating a sense of urgency in sales is a potent technique that can significantly shorten the sales cycle and encourage customers to commit. However, this sense of urgency must be genuine and not based on deceptive tactics. This law explores how to induce urgency and delves into why it's practical and essential in making sales. The Importance of Creating a Sense of Urgency

Urgency can compel action in ways that logical and emotional appeals might not. Here's why creating a sense of urgency is a critical sales technique:

1. Accelerates Decision-Making: Urgency helps overcome buyer procrastination and indecision by adding a time-sensitive element to the decision-making process.

2. Enhances the Value Proposition: Presenting your product or service as part of a limited opportunity can enhance its perceived value. Products often seem more valuable when available only for a limited time or in limited quantities.

3. Differentiate from Competitors: If your product is seen as valuable and in demand, it can stand out more distinctly from competitors in a crowded market.

4. Encourages Immediate Action: Urgency converts interest into action. It nudges customers from consideration to purchase, reducing the risk of them exploring alternatives or delaying a decision.

The Effectiveness Of Urgency Taps Into Several Psychological Triggers:

Scarcity: People tend to perceive scarce items as more valuable. Customers' desire to acquire the product increases When they believe an opportunity is limited.

Fear of Missing Out (FOMO): This social anxiety plays a role when customers see others making purchases and feel left out if they don't act quickly.

Commitment and Consistency: Once customers take a small step due to urgency, they are more likely to continue to commit to avoid cognitive dissonance.

Strategies To Create Urgency Ethically

Implementing urgency should always be done truthfully and transparently to maintain trust and credibility. Here are expanded strategies to induce urgency without compromising integrity:

1. Limited-Time Offers: Communicate time-bound offers such as discounts, bonuses, or special terms available for a limited period. Ensure these deadlines are real and enforced.

2. Limited Quantities Available: Highlight genuine limited availability of your product or service (due to high demand or exclusive batches). This factual statement about your inventory levels can create a strong push toward making a decision.

3. Special Editions: Offering special editions or limited releases of products can naturally create urgency due to the unique aspects of these offerings.

4. Customer Testimonials and Case Studies: Showcase examples of customers who have quickly benefited from acting promptly. This social proof can motivate others to make faster decisions.

5. Highlight Immediate Benefits: Emphasize what customers will gain immediately after purchasing. Immediate gratification is a powerful motivator.

6. Communicate the Consequences of Waiting: Honestly communicate potential downsides or missed opportunities if a decision is delayed. This can help customers weigh the benefits of immediate action.

Conclusion

When used correctly and ethically, creating a sense of urgency can be a valuable strategy in sales. It enhances the purchasing process, making it exciting, rewarding rather than stressful, or misleading. By developing urgency in your sales approach, you drive quicker decisions and improve sales efficiency, all while maintaining the trust and satisfaction of your customers. Ethical urgency respects the customer's ability to make an informed choice, reinforcing their confidence in the buying process and your integrity as a seller.

LAW 19: EMPHASIZE THE VALUE PROPOSITION

In sales, the value proposition is the cornerstone of every successful pitch. It clearly defines why customers should choose your product or service over competitors. This law focuses on articulating a compelling value proposition and provides strategies for emphasizing it effectively to ensure your customers understand the unique benefits and value they will receive.

A Well-Defined Value Proposition Is Critical Because It:

1. Clarifies Your Offering: It briefly explains what your product or service does and why it helps the customer.

2. Differentiates Your Product: It highlights what makes your offering unique and why it stands out in the market, helping customers understand why they should prefer it over others.

3. Increases Customer Engagement: A compelling value proposition grabs attention and engages potential buyers, making them more likely to consider your offering seriously.

4. Fosters Customer Loyalty: By delivering on your value proposition, you build trust and satisfaction, essential for

customer retention and loyalty.

5. Supports Premium Pricing: When the perceived value is high, customers are often willing to pay a premium, enhancing your profitability.

Crafting And Emphasizing Your Value Proposition To Effectively Communicate Your Value Proposition, Consider The Following Steps:

1. Identify Customer Needs and Challenges: Understand your target customers' needs, pain points, and challenges. This knowledge allows you to tailor your value proposition to address these issues directly.

2. Link Features to Benefits: Clearly articulate how the features of your product or service translate into tangible benefits for the customer. Don't just list features; explain how these features improve the customer's life or business.

3. Highlight Unique Differentiators: Identify what sets your offering apart from the competition and emphasize these points in your value proposition. Whether it's superior technology, better customer service, or unique design, ensure these differentiators are front and center.

4. Use Clear and Concise Language: Your value proposition should be straightforward and easily understood. Avoid jargon and complex language; simplicity ensures your message is

accessible to all potential buyers.

5. Reinforce with Social Proof: Support your value proposition with testimonials, case studies, and third-party reviews. Social proof can substantiate your claims and make your value proposition more credible.

6. Continuously Test and Refine: Market needs and competitive landscapes can change. Regularly test your value proposition with different segments of your target market and refine it based on feedback and evolving market conditions.

Conclusion

Emphasizing the value proposition effectively is not just about stating what your product or service does—it's about communicating its unique value in a way that resonates with your target audience. A compelling value proposition can be the difference between a prospective customer choosing your offering over a competitor's. Focusing on the benefits that directly address the customers' needs and differentiating your product in the market can enhance customer engagement, increase conversions, and build a loyal customer base.

LAW 20: USE PSYCHOLOGICAL PRINCIPLES

Understanding and applying psychological principles in sales can dramatically improve your ability to influence customer behavior and increase the effectiveness of your sales strategies. This law explores the key psychological concepts that can be leveraged in sales, explaining how they work and why they are crucial for persuading customers and closing deals.

The Application Of Psychology In Sales Is Foundational Because It Taps Into Subconscious Triggers That Influence Buying Behavior. Here's Why Integrating Psychological Principles Is Critical:

1. Enhances Persuasion: Understanding how and why people make decisions allows you to tailor your sales approaches to align with these intrinsic behaviors and preferences.

2. Builds Deeper Connections: By appealing to psychological needs such as security, belonging, or esteem, you can forge stronger emotional connections with customers.

3. Increases Effectiveness of Communications: Knowing what resonates psychologically with people helps craft messages that capture attention and motivate action.

4. Drives Customer Loyalty: Utilizing psychological principles to meet not just the overt but also the covert needs of your customers can foster loyalty and increase customer lifetime value.

5. Facilitates Better Customer Experiences: By anticipating and understanding customer reactions, you can design more satisfying experiences likely to result in positive outcomes.

Here Are Several Psychological Principles Are Particularly Effective In Sales Contexts:

1. Reciprocity: People feel obliged to give back to others who have given to them. In sales, this might mean providing something of value upfront—like a free trial or a helpful resource—thus increasing the likelihood of a reciprocated action, such as a purchase.

2. Commitment and Consistency: Once people commit to something, they are more likely to follow through to maintain consistency. Sales strategies can leverage this by securing small initial commitments that lead to larger ones.

3. Social Proof: People often look to the behavior of others to determine their own. Showcasing testimonials, customer reviews, and case studies can validate your offering and encourage others to follow suit.

4. Authority: Being seen as an expert or authority in your field can significantly sway buying decisions. This can be achieved by demonstrating knowledge, experience, and credibility through various forms of content like articles, speaking engagements, and expert endorsements.

5. Liking: People are likelier to buy from someone they like. Building rapport, finding common ground, and being genuinely friendly can make a substantial difference.

6. Scarcity: Items perceived as scarce or in limited supply are valued more highly than those readily available. Highlighting the exclusivity or limited availability of a product can spur purchases.

To Effectively Use Psychological Principles In Your Sales Approach, Consider These Steps:

1. Understand Your Audience: Deeply research and understand the psychological drivers of your target audience. What are their needs, fears, desires, and behaviors?

2. Tailor Communications: Use the insights from your audience research to craft messages that resonate on a psychological level.

3. Train Regularly: Continuously train yourself and your sales

team on the fundamentals of psychology in sales. Regularly update training to include the latest research and insights.

4. Measure and Adapt: Constantly test and measure your psychologically informed strategies' effectiveness, and adapt based on what is most effective.

Conclusion

Leveraging psychological principles in sales isn't about manipulation; it's about understanding human behavior to create win-win situations where customers feel their needs are met, and sales teams achieve their goals. By integrating these principles thoughtfully and ethically into your sales strategies, you can significantly enhance the effectiveness of your interactions and increase your overall sales success.

OVERVIEW OF COMMUNICATION AND PERSUASION

Part Four of "The 48 Laws of Sales" dives into the nuanced art of communication and the strategic application of persuasive techniques in sales. This section will equip you with advanced tools for effectively engaging customers, understanding their needs, and influencing their decision-making processes.

Overview

This section focuses on the critical aspects of sales communication and persuasion, with each law offering targeted strategies for enhancing how you interact with potential and existing customers. The aim is to improve your ability to communicate, persuade, and deepen your understanding of the psychological underpinnings that influence buyer behavior.

Core Themes

Tailoring Sales Pitches: Customizing your approach to suit various buyer types and situations.

Employing Storytelling: Leveraging narrative techniques to create engaging and memorable sales presentations.

Creating Urgency: Using ethical strategies to prompt quicker decision-making.

Emphasizing Value: Clearly articulating the value proposition to highlight the unique benefits of your products or services.

Utilizing Psychological Principles: Applying vital psychological insights to enhance persuasion and influence customer perceptions.

Integration Of Exercises And Scenarios

Law 16: Tailor Your Sales Pitch

Exercise: Develop different sales pitches tailored to at least three customer profiles based on their unique needs and preferences.

Scenario: A potential client is highly analytical and detail-oriented. Prepare a customized pitch that focuses on data and detailed specifications.

Law 17: Use Storytelling to Engage

Exercise: Create a story that encapsulates the core benefits of your product, incorporating real-life success stories.

Scenario: During a sales meeting, you notice the client losing interest. Script a compelling story that re-engages them and highlights the product's impact.

Law 18: Create a Sense of Urgency

Exercise: Practice crafting limited-time offer announcements that are both compelling and honest.

Scenario: You're launching a new product and want to maximize early sales. Design a campaign that ethically creates urgency.

Law 19: Emphasize the Value Proposition

Exercise: Write down your product's value proposition in a sentence, then expand this into a full presentation that addresses potential objections.

Scenario: A client is considering several options. Prepare a presentation that clearly outlines why your solution offers the best value.

Law 20: Use Psychological Principles

Exercise: Study and apply principles such as reciprocity and scarcity in your sales scripts.

Scenario: You're trying to close a deal with a hesitant client. Use psychological principles to influence their decision-making subtly.

Conclusion

Part Four of "The 48 Laws of Sales" emphasizes mastering communication and persuasion in sales. By engaging with the exercises and hypothetical scenarios provided, you will enhance your ability to connect with clients, understand their needs, and effectively guide them toward favorable decisions. These skills are essential for any sales professional looking to excel in a competitive marketplace and build lasting customer relationships.

PART FIVE: EMOTIONAL INTELLIGENCE AND INTERPERSONAL SKILLS

LAW 21: DEVELOP EMOTIONAL INTELLIGENCE

Emotional intelligence is the ability to recognize, understand, and manage one's own emotions as well as the emotions of others. In sales, emotional intelligence is a critical skill that can significantly enhance customer communication, negotiation, and relationship-building. This law explores why emotional intelligence is crucial in sales and offers strategies to effectively develop and utilize this skill. Emotional intelligence can transform how you interact with clients, leading to more successful outcomes.

Here Are Several Reasons Why Emotional Intelligence Is Essential In Sales:

1. Enhances Communication: High emotional intelligence enables you to communicate more effectively by understanding what to say and how to say it to resonate with your audience emotionally.

2. Builds Stronger Relationships: You can build more profound, trusting relationships by being aware of and responsive to clients' emotional needs and cues.

3. Improves Conflict Resolution: Emotional intelligence helps you handle conflicts constructively, turning potentially harmful situations into opportunities to build credibility and trust.

4. Increases Sales Effectiveness: Emotional intelligence allows you to understand better and align with customer motivations, potentially leading to more persuasive and successful sales pitches.

5. Supports Team Collaboration: High emotional intelligence benefits client interactions, working effectively with colleagues, and managing team dynamics.

Ways To Develop Emotional Intelligence

Developing your emotional intelligence involves a commitment to continuous learning and self-improvement. Here are some practical ways to enhance your emotional intelligence:

1. Self-awareness: Regularly reflect on your emotions and reactions. Journaling or meditation can be helpful practices to increase self-awareness. Understanding your emotional triggers and responses is the first step in managing them effectively.

2. Self-regulation: Once you know your emotions, work on regulating them. Techniques such as deep breathing, pausing before responding, and thinking through consequences can help maintain emotional control, especially in high-stakes situations.

3. Empathy: Actively practice empathy by seeing things from the customer's perspective. Listen attentively to their concerns

and respond thoughtfully. Improving your empathy skills can enhance your ability to connect with clients on an emotional level.

4. Social Skills: Work on developing strong interpersonal skills. This includes learning to communicate clearly, listen effectively, tactfully, and respectfully negotiate and persuade.

5. Motivation: Cultivate your intrinsic motivation to succeed in your role. Setting personal goals, seeking feedback, and celebrating small wins can help maintain high levels of motivation, which is contagious to clients and colleagues.

Conclusion

Developing emotional intelligence is not just about enhancing your ability to understand and manage emotions; it's about using that understanding to create better interactions, build stronger relationships, and achieve more effective sales outcomes. Investing in your emotional skills equips you with the tools needed to succeed in sales and all areas of life. High emotional intelligence is linked to better job performance, greater personal well-being, and improved leadership skills. As you continue to develop your emotional intelligence, you'll find that your capacity to influence and lead in sales will grow significantly, driving both personal and professional success.

LAW 22: MANAGE STRESS EFFECTIVELY

In the high-pressure sales world, stress is often an unavoidable part of the job. However, managing this stress effectively is crucial for your well-being and peak professional performance. This law examines the impact of stress on sales and offers practical methods for managing stress to ensure it doesn't hinder your success.

Effective Stress Management Is Vital In Sales For Several Reasons:

1. Maintains High Performance: Chronic stress can impair cognitive functions such as decision-making, problem-solving, and memory, which are essential for successful sales.

2. Enhances Emotional Intelligence: Managing stress improves emotional regulation, helping you maintain professionalism and empathy with clients even under pressure.

3. Prevents Burnout: Continuous unmanaged stress can lead to burnout, which might cause disengagement from work, reduced productivity, and even severe health issues.

4. Promotes Better Client Relationships: A stressed salesperson can inadvertently pass on stress to clients, potentially harming

relationships and trust.

5. Supports Overall Health: Chronic stress is linked to numerous health problems, including heart disease, diabetes, and depression. Managing stress effectively promotes better health, allowing you to remain focused and energetic.

Seven Ways To Manage Stress Effectively

1. Regular Exercise: Engage in physical activities that you enjoy, whether it's going to the gym, jogging, or playing a sport. Exercise is a proven stress reliever that improves your overall health and gives you a break from the work environment.

2. Mindfulness and Meditation: Practice mindfulness techniques to develop a greater awareness of the present moment. This can help decrease anxiety and feelings of stress by focusing your mind and calming your body.

3. Proper Time Management: Organize your schedule and prioritize tasks. Use tools like calendars and to-do lists to avoid last-minute rushes. Effective time management can significantly reduce work-related stress by making your day more manageable and predictable.

4. Healthy Eating Habits: Maintain a diet that supports your energy levels throughout the day. Avoid excessive caffeine and sugar, which can lead to energy crashes that compound stress.

5. Adequate Sleep: Ensure you get enough restful sleep each night. Sleep deprivation can exacerbate stress, reduce resilience, and impact your ability to handle daily challenges effectively.

6. Set Realistic Goals: Set achievable goals and break tasks into smaller steps. Celebrate small victories along the way to motivate yourself and reduce feeling overwhelmed.

7. Seek Support: Don't hesitate to seek support from colleagues, mentors, or professionals when needed. Sharing your experiences and challenges can help you gain perspective and find solutions to reduce stress.

Conclusion

Managing stress effectively is essential for maintaining optimal performance in sales. By implementing these strategies, you can reduce the negative impacts of tension and enhance your ability to engage positively with clients and colleagues. Remember, the goal is not to eliminate stress—often impossible—but to manage it to preserve your health and enhance your performance. Adopting these practices improves sales outcomes and contributes to a healthier, more satisfying professional life.

LAW 23: CULTIVATE A POSITIVE MINDSET

In the competitive and often unpredictable field of sales, maintaining a positive mindset is not just beneficial—it's essential. A positive attitude helps navigate the ups and downs of the sales process, driving persistence and fostering resilience. This law explores the importance of cultivating a positive mindset, how it affects your sales performance and strategies for developing and maintaining it.

A Positive Mindset Can Transform Your Approach To Sales, Leading To Numerous Benefits:

1. Enhances Resilience: Sales professionals frequently face rejection and setbacks. A positive mindset helps you see these challenges as opportunities for growth rather than failures.

2. Boosts Performance: Studies have shown that positivity increases productivity and performance. You're more likely to achieve better results when you enthusiastically approach your tasks.

3. Improves Problem-Solving: A positive attitude enhances creativity and the ability to think critically. This is crucial in sales, where you often must find innovative solutions for your clients' problems.

4. Fosters Stronger Relationships: Positivity is contagious. You can build more effective and enduring relationships with clients and colleagues by cultivating a positive mindset.

5. Supports Mental and Physical Health: Positive thinking can reduce stress and improve overall well-being, keeping you energized and focused. Developing and maintaining a positive mindset requires intentional practice.

Here Are Effective Strategies To Cultivate Positivity In Your Sales Career

1. Practice Gratitude: Regularly reflect on what you're grateful for. A gratitude journal can help you focus on the positive aspects of your life and work, even on tough days.

2. Set Realistic Goals: Establish achievable goals to avoid feeling overwhelmed. Celebrate when you meet these goals to reinforce positive feelings about your accomplishments.

3. Embrace Positive Affirmations: Positive affirmations reinforce confidence and reduce negative thoughts. Repeat affirmations that focus on your strengths and goals.

4. Learn from Rejections: View rejections not as failures but as learning opportunities. Analyze what went wrong, adjust your approach, and move forward with new insights.

5. Surround Yourself with Positivity: Engage with positive influences, whether they're colleagues who uplift you or motivational materials that inspire you. Avoid negativity, especially from those who undermine your goals.

6. Maintain a Healthy Work-Life Balance: Ensure you have time to relax and enjoy life outside work. A healthy balance can prevent burnout and maintain your overall positivity.

7. Visualize Success: Spend time visualizing successful outcomes. This practice can increase your confidence and help manifest these successes in reality.

Conclusion

Cultivating a positive mindset is a powerful tool in sales. It enables you to approach each day and each challenge with a constructive attitude, driving better results and more satisfying interactions. By actively maintaining positivity, you enhance your professional performance and contribute to your well-being and happiness. Remember, a positive mindset in sales isn't about ignoring the challenges—it's about facing them with the right attitude and turning potential obstacles into stepping stones for success.

LAW 24: ENHANCE YOUR PRESENTATION SKILLS

Practical presentation skills are essential in sales, as they directly influence how potential clients perceive you and your product. Delivering clear, compelling, and persuasive presentations can set you apart in a competitive market. This law explores the importance of presentation skills and outlines practical steps to enhance your ability in this critical area.

Strong Presentation Skills Are Crucial For Several Reasons:

1. First Impressions Count: Your presentation is often the first substantial interaction a potential client has with your product or service. A strong presentation can make a lasting impression.

2. Clear Communication: Good presentation skills help you communicate your message clearly and effectively, ensuring your audience understands your value proposition.

3. Persuasion and Influence: The ability to persuade and influence is at the heart of sales. Effective presentations can sway decision-makers and drive sales results.

4. Professionalism: Strong presentation skills reflect your professionalism and your company's credibility.

5. Competitive Edge: In competitive markets, the ability to deliver outstanding presentations can differentiate you from competitors.

Improving Your Presentation Skills Is A Continual Process. Here Are Essential Steps To Develop And Refine These Skills:

1. Understand Your Audience: Know who you are presenting to before crafting your presentation. What are their needs, challenges, and pain points? Tailor your presentation to address these elements directly.

2. Structure Your Presentation Effectively: Organize your presentation with a clear beginning, middle, and end. Start with a solid opening to grab attention, present your main points in the middle, and end with a compelling call to action.

3. Practice Clear and Concise Communication: Use simple, jargon-free language. Be concise but informative. Ensure your presentation is easy to follow and all technical terms are explained.

4. Develop Visual Aids: Use visual aids like slides, charts, and videos to support your message. Ensure these visuals are high quality and not overly cluttered. They should enhance your presentation, not detract from it.

5. Master Verbal and Non-Verbal Communication: Pay attention to your tone of voice, pacing, and body language. All these elements should convey confidence and enthusiasm.

6. Rehearse: Practice your presentation multiple times. Rehearse alone or with a trusted colleague in front of a mirror. Use feedback to make adjustments.

7. Learn from Each Presentation: After each presentation, reflect on what went well and what could be improved. Consider asking for feedback from your audience or recording your presentation to review later.

8. Stay Updated on Presentation Tools and Trends: Keep up-to-date with the latest presentation tools and trends, such as new software or techniques to engage your audience more effectively.

Conclusion

Enhancing your presentation skills is a powerful way to boost your sales effectiveness. By delivering clear, persuasive, and professional presentations, you communicate the value of your offerings more effectively and build trust and credibility with your audience. Continuous improvement in this area can lead to better sales outcomes and a more robust professional reputation. Invest time in developing these skills to become a more successful salesperson.

LAW 25: ADAPT SALES STRATEGIES TO CUSTOMER TYPES

Understanding that not all customers are the same is crucial for developing effective sales strategies. Each customer type has unique needs, preferences, and decision-making processes. This law emphasizes the importance of recognizing these differences and adapting your sales approach to maximize your effectiveness and increase your sales success.

Adapting Your Sales Strategies To Different Customer Types Is Important Because:

1. Enhances Customer Engagement: Tailored strategies ensure your approach resonates with each customer's interests and needs, leading to higher engagement.

2. Improves Customer Satisfaction: When customers feel understood, and their needs are addressed, their satisfaction increases, enhancing the likelihood of repeat business and referrals.

3. Increases Conversion Rates: A sales approach that aligns with the customer's buying behavior and preferences is more likely to result in a sale.

4. Builds Stronger Relationships: By showing that you

understand and value the unique characteristics of each customer, you build stronger, more trusting relationships.

Key Customer Types And Tailored Strategies

Here are some common customer types and strategies for effectively selling to each:

1. The Analytical Customer:

Characteristics: Loves data, details, and in-depth analysis. Makes decisions based on logic and thorough evaluation.

Strategies: Provide comprehensive data, detailed case studies, and ROI calculations. Be prepared for detailed questions and ensure your information is accurate and well-supported.

2. The Relationship-Oriented Customer:

Characteristics: Values, personal connection, and trust. Prefers to buy from salespeople they like and trust.

Strategies: Focus on building a solid rapport. Engage in meaningful conversations that go beyond business. Highlight testimonials and stories of long-term customer satisfaction.

3. The Value-Oriented Customer:

Characteristics: Focuses on the overall value rather than just price. I am interested in quality, durability, and cost-effectiveness.

Strategies: Emphasize the long-term benefits and cost savings of your product. Use comparisons to show how your offering provides the best value over time.

4. The Impulsive Customer:

Characteristics: Makes quick decisions based on emotions and immediate gratification.

Strategies: Create a sense of urgency. Use compelling visuals and emotional appeals to make your product seem irresistible. Offer limited-time deals to encourage quick action.

5. The Innovator Customer:

Characteristics: Always looking for the latest and greatest. Values innovation and being a trendsetter.

Strategies: Highlight the newest features and cutting-edge aspects of your product. Showcase how adopting your product puts them ahead of the curve.

Conclusion

Adapting your sales strategies to match the specific types of customers you encounter is crucial for sales success. By understanding and addressing each customer type's diverse needs and preferences, you can craft more effective sales pitches, build better relationships, and ultimately close more deals. Learning about customer behavior and preferences will keep your sales strategies adequate and relevant, ensuring long-term success in a competitive market.

OVERVIEW OF EMOTIONAL INTELLIGENCE AND INTERPERSONAL SKILLS

Part Five focuses on developing and applying emotional intelligence and interpersonal skills in sales. These skills are essential for building meaningful relationships with clients, understanding their needs, and effectively communicating your message. This section provides a cohesive integration of laws that guide you in enhancing these skills through practical exercises and scenarios.

Law 21: Develop Emotional Intelligence

Core Principle: Recognize and manage your emotions and the emotions of others to improve engagement and communication.

Exercise: Practice active listening in your interactions to better understand and respond to the emotions of others.

Hypothetical Scenario: You notice a long-term client seems unusually curt and disinterested during a presentation. How would you use emotional intelligence to handle and uncover the underlying issues?

Law 22: Master Non-Verbal Communication

Core Principle: Use non-verbal cues effectively to communicate confidence and sincerity.

Exercise: Record a role-playing session with a coworker or someone you know, where you practice your sales presentation. Analyze your body language, eye contact, and tone of voice to identify areas for improvement. Focus on how your non-verbal cues can better convey confidence and engage your audience.

Hypothetical Scenario: During a negotiation, you observe the client folding their arms and leaning back whenever you discuss pricing. How would you adjust your non-verbal communication to foster a more open and positive atmosphere?

Law 23: Practice Active Listening

Core Principle: Engage fully with clients by listening to understand, not just to respond.

Exercise: In your next sales meeting, focus entirely on the client's words without planning your response. After the meeting, summarize their key points to ensure understanding.

Hypothetical Scenario: A client expresses several concerns about proceeding with a purchase. Demonstrate how you would use active listening to address each problem and reassure the client.

Law 24: Enhance Your Presentation Skills

Core Principle: Deliver clear, persuasive, and professional presentations to communicate your offerings' value effectively.

Exercise: Develop a new sales presentation incorporating storytelling and vital closing techniques. Present it to a peer for feedback.

Hypothetical Scenario: You're asked to pitch a complex product to a new customer with little technical knowledge. Plan how you would simplify your presentation to make it accessible and engaging.

Law 25: Adapt Sales Strategies to Customer Types

Core Principle: Tailor your sales approach to fit different customer types' diverse behaviors and preferences.

Exercise: Create profiles for different customer types you encounter and develop tailored strategies for each.

Hypothetical Scenario: You are dealing with a highly analytical customer who has resisted making a quick decision. Outline your strategy for presenting data and evidence to meet their needs and help close the sale.

Conclusion Of Part Five

This part of the book equips you with essential techniques for leveraging emotional intelligence and refining interpersonal skills, which are crucial for navigating the complexities of modern sales environments. The exercises and scenarios included are designed to challenge and improve your understanding of interacting with clients effectively, enhancing your personal growth and professional success.

PART SIX: NEGOTIATION AND CLOSING

LAW 26: NEGOTIATE WIN-WIN SOLUTIONS

Effective negotiation isn't about overpowering the opponent but achieving harmony and balance. A salesperson understands that both parties feel victorious during the most successful talks. This is the essence of creating win-win solutions. When everyone wins, a deal is concluded, and a foundation is laid for long-term relationships, transforming customers into lifetime clients.

The Philosophy Of Win-Win

The concept of win-win negotiations challenges traditional competitive negotiation tactics, often leading to win-lose or lose-lose outcomes. Instead, win-win negotiation encourages a mindset where the salesperson seeks to understand and satisfy the needs of both parties involved. This philosophy is rooted in empathy, mutual respect, and collaboration. It demands that you, as a salesperson, step into your client's shoes and ask yourself: "What does a good deal look like for them?"

Understanding Client Needs

The first step towards crafting win-win solutions is a deep understanding of your client's needs, desires, and pressures. This understanding comes from meticulous research and active listening. During conversations with clients, focus not only on what is said but also on what is unsaid. Please observe non-verbal cues and ask probing questions to encourage clients to open up about their needs.

Building Trust Through Transparency

Transparency is vital in win-win negotiations. You build trust by being open about your limitations and honest about what you can offer. Clients appreciate transparency as it steers the conversation away from manipulative tactics and towards mutual gains. When clients trust you, they are more likely to share their constraints and needs, facilitating a better solution.

The Art Of Creative Problem Solving

Win-win negotiations thrive on creative problem-solving. This involves thinking outside the traditional confines of the deal and exploring alternative ways to satisfy both parties' needs. For instance, if price is a sticking point, you might focus on adding value through service enhancements, flexible delivery options, or extended warranties instead of reducing the price.

Effective Communication Strategies

Effective communication is the backbone of negotiation. It involves clearly articulating your points and active listening to understand the client's perspective. Use affirming language to show you know and respect the client's needs and preferences. Phrases like "I see what you mean," "It makes sense that you'd need that," and "Let's work together to solve this" can set a collaborative tone.

The Role Of Empathy

Empathy plays a crucial role in achieving win-win outcomes. It allows you to genuinely understand the impact of the negotiation from the client's viewpoint. This insight can be pivotal in adjusting your approach and offerings to align more closely with the client's expectations and conditions.

The Importance Of Patience

Patience is a strategic asset in negotiations. Rushing to close the deal can lead to overlooking important details or making concessions that could harm your position. Take the time to explore all angles and options, ensuring that the solution developed genuinely benefits all involved.

Long-Term Thinking

Win-win is not just a strategy but a long-term approach. By focusing on the client's success as part of your own, you foster a relationship that can yield repeated business and referrals. Long-term thinking involves considering how the negotiation will affect future interactions with the client and their perception of your business.

Handling Objections Gracefully

Objections are inevitable in sales negotiations, but addressing them gracefully can turn potential setbacks into opportunities to create a win-win solution. Listen carefully, validate the client's concerns, and respond with thoughtful, tailored solutions. This shows that you value the client's satisfaction and are committed to finding an agreeable resolution.

Closing With Confidence

When it comes time to close the deal, do so with confidence. Summarize the agreement's benefits, emphasizing how they meet the client's needs. Reaffirm the value the client gets and express your commitment to supporting them post-sale. A confident close sets the tone for the client relationship moving forward.

Continuous Improvement

Lastly, every negotiation is a learning opportunity. Reflect on what went well and what could be improved. This continuous improvement mindset will enhance your ability to create win-win solutions in the future, increasing your effectiveness as a salesperson and strengthening your client relationships.

LAW 27: ALWAYS FOLLOW UP

Following up with customers after initial interactions, presentations, or purchases is fundamental to successful sales strategies. This law explores why consistent follow-up is essential and provides guidelines on effectively engaging with customers post-interaction to enhance relationships and boost sales.

Adequate Follow-Up Is Crucial For Several Reasons

1. Strengthens Customer Relationships: Regular follow-up demonstrates to customers that you value their business and are committed to their satisfaction, fostering a sense of trust and loyalty.

2. Increases Sales Opportunities: Follow-up interactions can reveal additional customer needs that may lead to further sales or upselling opportunities.

3. Improves Customer Retention: You enhance customer retention rates by staying in touch and addressing any issues promptly. Satisfied customers are more likely to return and recommend your services to others.

4. Gather Valuable Feedback: Following up provides an opportunity to collect feedback about your products, services,

and the overall customer experience, which is vital for continuous improvement.

5. Enhances Brand Reputation: Consistent and thoughtful follow-up contributes to a positive brand image by showing that your company cares about its customers beyond the initial sale.

To Maximize The Benefits Of Following Up With Customers, Consider These Strategies

1. Timeliness: Timing is crucial in follow-up. Reach out soon after an interaction while the experience remains fresh in the customer's mind. Determine the optimal timing based on the type of interaction—for instance, shortly after purchase or within a few days following a service inquiry.

2. Personalization: Tailor your follow-up to the specific customer and situation. Use details from the initial interaction to personalize communications, making customers feel recognized and valued.

3. Use Multiple Channels: Depending on the customer's preferences, utilize various channels for follow-up, including email, phone calls, text messages, or even direct mail. This multi-channel approach ensures you are reaching the customer most effectively.

4. Provide Value in Every Interaction: Ensure each follow-up adds value. This could be helpful information related to their

purchase, tips on better use of your product, or relevant offers that meet their ongoing needs.

5. Ask for Feedback: Always include a request for feedback in your follow-up. This shows that you are open to learning and improving, and it gives customers a chance to express any concerns or satisfaction.

6. Set Up Next Steps: If applicable, use follow-up communications to set up the next steps. This could involve scheduling a meeting, reminding customers about renewal dates, or informing them about upcoming promotions.

Conclusion

Following up is not just a courtesy; it's a strategic component of effective sales and customer service processes. By consistently reaching out and engaging with your customers after initial interactions, you increase the chances of repeat business and build a foundation for long-term customer loyalty and satisfaction. Regular and thoughtful follow-ups can turn a one-time buyer into a lifelong customer and advocate for your brand.

LAW 28: RECOGNIZE BUYING SIGNALS

Recognizing buying signals—subtle and overt cues that indicate a customer's readiness to purchase—is a crucial skill for any salesperson. This law explores various buying signals and guides how to respond to these cues effectively to close sales.

Identifying Buying Signals Promptly Allows You To

1. Respond Appropriately: Tailor your approach based on the customer's readiness, increasing the likelihood of closing a sale.

2. Maximize Sales Opportunities: By recognizing and acting on buying signals, you can capitalize on the moment of highest customer interest.

3. Enhance Customer Experience: Responding accurately to buying signals shows that you understand and respect the customer's purchase process, enhancing their overall experience and satisfaction.

4. Increase Efficiency: Knowing when a customer is ready to buy helps you allocate your time and resources more effectively, focusing your efforts where they are most likely to yield results.

Examples Of Buying Signals And How To Respond

Buying signals can vary widely but typically fall into verbal and non-verbal categories. Here are some common examples and suggestions on how to respond:

Verbal Buying Signals

Questions about Specifics: If a customer starts asking detailed questions about pricing, features, or availability, it often means they are considering a purchase.

Response: Provide clear, concise answers and begin transitioning the conversation towards making a purchase decision, such as discussing payment options or delivery details.

Positive Statements: Expressions of approval or positive comments about your product or service can indicate interest.

Response: Reinforce these positive sentiments by agreeing and offering additional reasons why the product is a good fit for their needs.

Non-Verbal Buying Signals

Nodding or Leaning In Physical engagement or nodding while discussing specific features can indicate interest.

Response: Acknowledge this interest by expanding on the benefits of the features they seem interested in and suggest taking the next step towards purchase.

Prolonged Handling of the Product: If in a physical store, extended handling or examining of the product often shows buying intent.

Response: Confirm the product's suitability for their needs and encourage the decision by discussing the ease of purchase and satisfaction guarantees.

Decision-Making Cues

Consulting with Peers or Partners During a Meeting:

When a customer consults with others in their group or asks for opinions during your presentation, it often indicates a collective consideration towards a decision.

Response: Offer to address any questions the group might have collectively and present options that cater to the consensus, emphasizing how your product or service meets their shared requirements.

Request for Customization or Modifications: When a customer inquires about customizing a product or asks about specific modifications, it's a strong indicator of serious interest.

Response: Discuss the customization options in detail, highlighting how these modifications can better meet their specific needs or preferences.

Conclusion

Recognizing and responding to buying signals effectively is vital to successful sales. It requires attentiveness, the ability to interpret customer actions and words accurately, and the decisiveness to act on these signals. By honing this skill, you can significantly improve your sales performance, close deals faster, and build better customer relationships, ultimately enhancing customer satisfaction and sales success.

LAW 29: OVERCOME PRICE OBJECTIONS

Price objections are among the most common challenges sales professionals face. They often signify concerns about cost and more profound questions about the value and return on investment. This law focuses on strategies to build value effectively and prepare through role-playing to ensure sales professionals can confidently and effectively overcome price objections. Price objections do not necessarily signal disinterest or the end of a sales opportunity. Instead, they can provide a pivotal moment to deepen a customer's understanding and appreciation of your product's value.

Overcoming These Objections Is Crucial Because

1. Enhances Customer Understanding: Addressing price objections effectively helps clarify the benefits and the unique value proposition of your product or service.

2. Builds Trust: Customers are more likely to trust sales professionals who can competently and confidently address their concerns, including pricing-related concerns.

3. Improves Sales Success: Successfully overcoming price objections often leads to closing deals, which might otherwise be lost.

4. Strengthens Relationship: By engaging deeply in value, you develop a stronger relationship with the customer, setting the stage for future business and referrals.

Building Value Is A Proactive Strategy To Preempt And Counter Price Objections. Here Are Detailed Ways To Enhance Perceived Value

1. Highlight Quality and ROI: Focus on the quality and durability of your product or service and how these lead to long-term savings or high return on investment. Use data and examples to back up your claims.

2. Demonstrate Differentiation: Clearly articulate what differentiates your product from competitors. This could be innovation, better customer service, additional features, or superior performance. Make it clear why these differentiators justify a higher price point.

3. Tailor Benefits to Specific Needs: Connect the features of your product directly to the unique needs or pain points of the customer. Show how your solution addresses these needs more effectively than alternative options.

4. Utilize Testimonials and Case Studies: Share stories and data from other satisfied customers who thought the product was worth the price. Real-world examples can powerfully illustrate value.

Role-Playing To Prepare For Price Objections

Role-playing is a practical training technique to prepare for handling price objections. It helps sales professionals practice responses in a controlled environment, building confidence and refining their approach. Here's how to implement role-playing effectively:

1. Simulate Realistic Scenarios: Create scenarios that reflect everyday sales situations and potential objections you encounter. Use actual customer interactions as templates.

2. Practice a Variety of Responses: Develop and rehearse multiple strategies for responding to price objections. This could include justifying the price based on the product's features, comparing it with less effective but cheaper alternatives, and demonstrating long-term value.

3. Get Feedback: Use feedback from peers and trainers to improve your responses. Constructive criticism helps identify weaknesses in your pitch or areas where the value isn't communicated.

4. Refine and Repeat: Regular practice helps refine your approach. Make role-playing a regular part of sales training to improve the team's continuous handling of price objections.

Conclusion

Overcoming price objections is less about defending a cost and more about affirming value. It requires preparation, a deep understanding of your product's benefits, and the ability to communicate these effectively. By building value and employing regular role-playing exercises, sales professionals can enhance their ability to navigate price objections, leading to tremendous sales success and customer satisfaction. This proactive approach ensures that when price objections arise, they can be transformed into opportunities to reinforce the product's worth and solidify customer relationships.

LAW 30: BE A CONSULTANT, NOT A SALESPERSON

In today's sophisticated market, customers seek more than just products; they seek solutions and expertise. Transitioning from a traditional sales role to a consultant is crucial for modern sales professionals. This law outlines why adopting a consultative approach is beneficial and how it transforms interactions with customers, making them more productive and trusted.

The Importance Of Being A Consultant

Adopting a consultative approach in sales significantly changes how customers perceive and interact with you. Here are key reasons why being a consultant rather than just a salesperson is essential:

1. Builds Deeper Trust: Consultants are seen as experts who are there to help, not just to sell. This perception builds deeper trust between you and your clients.

2. Enhances Customer Satisfaction: By focusing on solving problems rather than pushing products, you align more closely with the customer's needs, leading to higher satisfaction.

3. Improves Customer Retention: Customers are more likely to return to a consultant who has successfully guided them

through complex decisions and provided real value.

4. Facilitates Higher Value Sales: As a consultant, you can often identify and create opportunities for upselling and cross-selling by addressing broader customer needs.

5. Strengthens Your Professional Reputation: Being seen as a knowledgeable consultant enhances your professional reputation, making you more attractive to customers and within your industry.

Here Are Practical Steps To Become More Of A Consultant And Less Of A Traditional Salesperson

1. Develop In-depth Product and Market Knowledge: A deep understanding of your products, services, and the market is fundamental. Stay updated with industry trends, common challenges, and emerging solutions so you can speak with authority and insight.

2. Focus on Problem Solving: Approach each customer interaction with the mindset of solving a problem. Ask probing questions to fully understand the challenges they face before recommending solutions.

3. Listen More Than You Speak: True consultants excel in listening. This allows you to gather essential information to guide your recommendations and show the customer that their needs and opinions are valued.

4. Tailor Your Communication: Customize your communication to each customer's context and needs. Avoid generic pitches; instead, present your solutions in a way that directly addresses the unique challenges or goals of the customer.

5. Provide Custom Solutions, Not Standard Products: Shift from selling standard products to creating customized solutions that deliver more value. This might involve combining products, adjusting service levels, or integrating innovative approaches tailored to specific customer requirements.

6. Educate Your Customers: Offer valuable information and education as part of your sales process. This could be through workshops, articles, webinars, or detailed guides that help the customer understand their needs better and how they can be met.

7. Follow Up Thoughtfully: Continue to provide support and advice after closing a sale. Regular follow-ups to assess how the solution works or could be improved reinforce your role as a consultant.

Conclusion

Transitioning from a traditional sales approach to a consultative role transforms how professionals engage with their clients, focusing on long-term relationships and mutual success. As a consultant, you position yourself as a trusted advisor that customers can rely on to guide them through complex decisions.

This enhances the sales process and leads to better customer and business outcomes, establishing a foundation for continued success and growth in your sales career.

OVERVIEW OF NEGOTIATION AND CLOSING

Part Six focuses on mastering the crucial stages of negotiation and closing in the sales process. This book section provides detailed insights and strategies for negotiating win-win solutions, following up diligently, recognizing buying signals, overcoming price objections, and adopting a consultative sales approach. Each law is supplemented with practical exercises and hypothetical scenarios to reinforce learning and application.

Law 26: Negotiate Win-Win Solutions

Core Principle: Strive for agreements that benefit both the seller and the buyer, enhancing long-term relationships.

Exercise: Role-play negotiation scenarios with colleagues, focusing on finding mutually beneficial outcomes.

Hypothetical Scenario: A client wants a lower price on a high-cost item. Negotiate by offering added value through service agreements or bundled products instead of lowering prices, maintaining profit margins while satisfying the client's needs.

Law 27: Always Follow Up

Core Principle: Consistent follow-up is crucial in nurturing customer relationships and ensuring satisfaction.

Exercise: Develop a follow-up schedule using CRM software for interactions, such as post-meeting, post-sale, and post-service inquiries.

Hypothetical Scenario: After a significant sale, the customer has not utilized the product to its full potential. Plan a follow-up strategy to offer additional training and support, reinforcing the value of their purchase.

Law 28: Recognize Buying Signals

Core Principle: Identifying subtle and explicit customer cues that indicate buying readiness can dramatically enhance closing rates.

Exercise: Create a checklist of standard buying signals and practice identifying these during sales calls or meetings.

Hypothetical Scenario: During a demonstration, a customer asks about product scalability and integration options. Respond by affirming these features and moving towards finalizing the sale, recognizing these questions as solid buying signals.

Law 29: Overcome Price Objections

Core Principle: Effectively address concerns about pricing by emphasizing value, not cost.

Exercise: Prepare and memorize a list of responses to common price objections that focus on your product's unique benefits and ROI.

Hypothetical Scenario: A potential client objects to pricing, citing cheaper alternatives. Demonstrate the superior value of your offering with a comparison chart showing long-term benefits and cost savings, aiming to shift the conversation from price to value.

Law 30: Be a Consultant, Not a Salesperson

Core Principle: Shift from selling to a consulting mindset, focusing on providing solutions rather than just pushing products.

Exercise: Conduct monthly reviews of client interactions to evaluate how effectively you adopted a consultative approach, focusing on problem-solving and tailored advice.

Hypothetical Scenario: A regular client mentions a new challenge they are facing. Instead of immediately suggesting a new product, engage in a detailed discussion to understand their needs fully, and then offer a customized solution that integrates seamlessly with the solutions you've provided previously.

Conclusion Of Part Six

This part of the book empowers sales professionals to refine their negotiation and closing skills through a strategic, thoughtful approach emphasizing understanding and meeting customer needs while achieving successful sales outcomes. The exercises and scenarios enhance your practical skills in these critical areas, ensuring you are well-prepared to handle various sales situations effectively.

PART SEVEN: SALES PLANNING AND ORGANIZATION

LAW 31: STAY ORGANIZED

Organization is a fundamental skill for sales professionals, directly impacting efficiency, effectiveness, and, ultimately, success in sales. This law explores the importance of staying organized and provides strategies to maintain an orderly approach to your sales activities.

Maintaining Organization In Sales Is Critical For Several Reasons

1. Enhances Productivity: An organized salesperson can manage their time and resources more effectively, ensuring they can handle multiple clients and projects without missing deadlines or opportunities.

2. Improves Customer Relationships: Organization helps you professionally manage customer interactions. Keeping track of customer details, previous interactions, and specific needs lets you personalize your communications and follow-ups, enhancing customer satisfaction.

3. Reduces Stress: Organization reduces the chaos of daily activities. Knowing exactly what needs to be done and when it needs to be done can lower stress levels and prevent burnout.

4. Increases Sales Opportunities: You can better identify and act

on sales opportunities with a well-organized approach. Tracking leads and sales stages effectively ensure no opportunities slip through the cracks.

5. Supports Accurate Forecasting and Reporting: Organization is vital to tracking sales metrics accurately, which is essential for forecasting future sales and reporting current performance to management.

Strategies to Stay Organized

To enhance your organizational skills in sales, consider the following strategies:

1. Utilize CRM Systems: Customer Relationship Management (CRM) systems are essential for tracking customer interactions, sales pipelines, and schedules. Ensure you use a CRM to its full potential by regularly updating information and using its features to automate tasks.

2. Develop a Daily Routine: Structure your day with a routine that allocates specific times for various activities, such as prospecting, following up on leads, and administrative tasks. Consistency in your daily routine can significantly enhance your productivity.

3. Prioritize Tasks: Use a system to prioritize your tasks based on urgency and importance. Techniques like the Eisenhower Box can help you decide which tasks to do immediately, schedule for

later, delegate, or eliminate.

4. Keep a Clean Workspace: A cluttered workspace can lead to a disorganized mind. Keep your physical and digital workspaces organized and free of unnecessary clutter. This includes your desktop, email inbox, and any physical files.

5. Set Clear Goals and Milestones: Clearly defined goals and milestones for each week or month can help you stay focused and organized. Review and adjust these goals regularly to stay aligned with overall sales targets.

6. Review and Plan Regularly: Review what was accomplished at the end of each day and prepare for the next day. This helps stay organized and maintain a clear focus on upcoming priorities.

Conclusion

Staying organized is not just about keeping your calendar and contacts in order; it's about maintaining a system that allows you to operate efficiently. For sales professionals, organization is directly tied to performance. By implementing robust organizational systems and habits, you ensure you can effectively meet the demands of a dynamic sales environment, leading to better performance outcomes, satisfied customers, and a successful sales career.

LAW 32: PRACTICE EFFECTIVE TIME MANAGEMENT

Time management is a critical skill for sales professionals, directly influencing productivity, stress levels, and overall success. Effective time management allows for better prioritization of tasks, a more precise focus during work hours, and, ultimately, more successful outcomes. This law guides you through starting with daily planning and gradually expanding to effective long-term time management.

Mastering Time Management Is Essential For Several Key Reasons

1. Maximizes Efficiency: Proper time management helps you accomplish more in less time by focusing on what's most important.

2. Reduces Stress: Knowing that you have a plan for tackling your tasks can significantly reduce stress associated with workload and deadlines.

3. Improves Work Quality: With adequate time allotted to each task, the quality of work improves as you're less likely to rush through assignments.

4. Enhances Professional Reputation: Being punctual and

consistently meeting deadlines enhances your reliability and professionalism in the eyes of colleagues and clients.

Here's How To Progressively Master Time Management

1. Start Small – Plan Your Day:

Begin each day by outlining a list of tasks to be completed. Prioritize these tasks based on urgency and importance.

Allocate specific time slots for each task. This technique, known as time blocking, helps deduce focused periods for important activities without the risk of overrunning into the time reserved for other tasks.

2. Expand to Weekly Planning:

Once you are comfortable with daily planning, start organizing your tasks weekly.

Review the upcoming week every Sunday, allocate time for each task, and adjust your plans based on priorities. Weekly planning allows for better handling of unexpected tasks and adjustments.

3. Plan Monthly and Annually:

Extend your planning to monthly and yearly goals. Set objectives you aim to achieve by the end of each month and year.

Break down these larger goals into smaller, manageable tasks you can schedule throughout the year.

Tips For Effective Time Management

1. Use Tools and Technology: Utilize calendars, task management apps, and reminders to keep track of your schedules and deadlines. Also, you can use an old-fashioned pen and paper

2. Learn to Say No: Understand your limits and avoid overcommitting. No to less critical tasks can free up time for more important duties.

3. Eliminate Distractions: Identify what distracts you during work and find ways to minimize these interruptions. This might involve setting times to check emails or using apps blocking distracting websites.

4. Review and Adjust Regularly: Review your progress towards your daily, weekly, monthly, and annual goals. Be flexible and willing to adjust your plans to accommodate new information or changing circumstances.

5. Take Breaks: Schedule short breaks between tasks to clear your mind and avoid burnout. These breaks can improve concentration and overall efficiency.

Conclusion

Effective time management doesn't happen overnight. It requires discipline, consistency, and a willingness to adapt and refine your methods. By starting small and gradually building up your planning skills from daily tasks to annual goals, you can achieve greater productivity and success in your sales career. Practice, persistence, and patience are crucial to mastering this essential skill.

LAW 33: SET AND REVIEW GOALS REGULARLY

Setting and regularly reviewing goals is crucial for driving sales success. This law underscores the significance of establishing clear, achievable goals and outlines strategies for maintaining momentum and accountability through consistent performance reviews.

Goal Setting In Sales Serves Multiple Essential Functions

1. Provides Direction: Clear goals give you a roadmap to follow, which can guide your daily activities and long-term planning.

2. Enhances Motivation: Well-defined goals can boost motivation by providing something concrete to strive for. Achieving these goals can increase satisfaction and drive.

3. Improves Performance: Regularly setting and reviewing goals helps you stay on track and make necessary adjustments, which can significantly improve your sales performance.

4. Facilitates Measurement of Success: Goals allow you to measure your progress and effectiveness, helping you understand what strategies work and where you need improvement.

To Ensure That Your Goals Are Practical And Achievable, Consider The Following Strategies

1. Be Specific: Clearly define what you want to achieve. Instead of setting a goal to "increase sales," set a specific target, such as "increase sales by 20% within the next quarter."

2. Make Them Measurable: Ensure that your goals can be quantified. This makes it easier to track progress and know when you have achieved them.

3. Ensure Relevance: Your goals should be relevant to your broader sales strategies and align with your personal and organizational objectives.

4. Set Time-Bound Targets: Assign a deadline to each goal to prevent tasks from being indefinitely postponed. This helps maintain a sense of urgency.

5. Keep Goals Achievable: While it's essential to be ambitious, your goals should also be within reach. Setting overly ambitious goals can lead to frustration and demotivation.

Daily And Incremental Goal Setting

In addition to setting broad, long-term goals, focus on daily and incremental targets:

Daily Sales Goals: If you want to make a sale daily, outline specific daily activities to help achieve this. For days when a sale isn't made, have a fallback plan to ensure productivity doesn't drop. For example, if no sale is achieved, make it a goal to make 100 calls and send 100 emails to potential clients. This keeps the momentum going and increases the chances of future sales.

Weekly Reviews: At the end of each week, review your achievements against your goals. This allows you to adjust your strategies and efforts for the coming week.

Tips For Regular Goal Review

1. Schedule Regular Review Sessions: Set a weekly or monthly time to review your goals and progress. Treat these sessions as mandatory appointments.

2. Adjust Goals as Needed: Be flexible with your goals. If you consistently miss targets despite your best efforts, adjusting them to more realistic levels might be necessary.

3. Celebrate Achievements: When you meet or exceed a goal, take the time to celebrate. This can be as simple as acknowledging your success or as elaborate as rewarding yourself with a small treat.

4. Learn from Misses: Analyze why specific goals were not met. Understanding what didn't work is critical to improving future

performance.

Conclusion

Setting and regularly reviewing goals is a dynamic process that requires commitment and flexibility. By establishing realistic, measurable, and time-bound goals and rigorously tracking your progress against these goals, you can enhance your effectiveness and efficiency in sales. Regular goal setting and review foster a proactive approach to sales, keeping you motivated and focused on achieving your highest potential.

LAW 34: PREPARE FOR EVERY SCENARIO

Preparation is vital to confidence and success. This law emphasizes the critical role of preparing for every potential scenario you might encounter during sales interactions. Role-playing is essential for this preparation, allowing you to anticipate and effectively respond to various customer objections and situations.

Importance Of Preparation In Sales

Preparation equips you to handle unexpected challenges and objections with ease and professionalism. Here's why thorough preparation is crucial:

1. **Boosts Confidence:** Being well-prepared increases your confidence during interactions, helping you present yourself and your product more effectively.

2. **Enhances Adaptability:** Preparation through role-playing various scenarios enhances your ability to adapt quickly to unexpected questions or objections from customers.

3. **Improves Persuasive Skills:** Regular practice in handling different sales situations sharpens your persuasive skills and your ability to close deals.

4. Reduces Anxiety: Knowing you have prepared for various scenarios can significantly reduce anxiety and stress, leading to more successful sales interactions.

Role-Playing For Sales Preparation

Role-playing is a practical tool to prepare for the dynamic nature of sales conversations. Here's how to implement role-playing effectively:

1. Compile a List of Common Objections: List all the objections you have encountered in past sales situations. Include common concerns about pricing, product features, competitors, and any other resistance you have faced.

2. Expand Your List: Ask colleagues or peers about objections they have encountered. Each salesperson might face unique challenges based on their approach and territory, providing a broader spectrum of scenarios to prepare for.

3. Develop Responses: For each objection on your list, develop a clear, concise, and persuasive response. These responses should address the objection and pivot back to the strengths of your product or service.

4. Role-Play Scenarios: Organize regular role-playing sessions with your colleagues. Take turns playing the role of the salesperson and the customer. The 'customer' should throw

different objections at the 'salesperson,' who should use their prepared responses.

5. Refine Your Techniques: Use feedback from these sessions to refine your responses and approaches. If specific objections pose difficulties, reevaluating and adjusting your responses may be necessary.

6. Incorporate Complex Scenarios: As you become more comfortable with primary objections, introduce more complex scenarios that combine multiple objections or involve highly skeptical or demanding customers.

Tips For Effective Role-Playing

Keep it Realistic: The more realistic the role-play, the better prepared you will be for actual sales interactions.

Record and Review: Recording role-playing sessions can provide insights that might be missed in the moment. Review these recordings to identify areas for improvement.

Continuous Learning: Sales scenarios evolve as new products, competitors, and market conditions emerge. Regularly update your list of objections and responses to reflect these changes.

Conclusion

Preparation through role-playing is an invaluable strategy in sales, equipping you to handle a wide range of customer interactions confidently and effectively. By anticipating potential objections and rehearsing your responses, you can significantly improve your ability to navigate complex sales dialogues and increase your overall success rate. This proactive approach ensures that you are not just reacting at the moment but are fully prepared to turn challenges into opportunities for closing sales.

LAW 35: MANAGE YOUR SALES PIPELINE

Effective sales pipeline management is crucial for maintaining a clear overview of potential deals at various sales process stages. This law provides practical tips and strategies to enhance pipeline management, ensuring you maximize opportunities and drive sales growth.

Importance Of Managing Your Sales Pipeline

A well-managed sales pipeline provides numerous benefits:

1. Enhances Visibility: Keeping your pipeline organized gives you a clear view of upcoming opportunities, current negotiations, and areas needing attention.

2. Improves Forecasting Accuracy: With a well-maintained pipeline, you can more accurately predict sales outcomes and revenue, which is crucial for strategic planning.

3. Increases Efficiency: Effective pipeline management helps prioritize efforts on the most promising leads, optimizing your time and resources.

4. Facilitates Better Resource Allocation: Understanding the

status of each deal allows you to allocate resources (like support from other teams) more effectively.

5. Drives Sales Growth: By actively managing your pipeline, you can push deals through to closure faster, driving sales growth and achieving targets.

Tips For Managing Your Sales Pipeline

Here are key strategies to effectively manage and optimize your sales pipeline:

1. Regularly Update and Cleanse the Pipeline:

Regularly update each lead's status and opportunity to reflect their current state accurately.

Remove stagnant leads or reclassify them based on updated interactions. This keeps your pipeline clean and focused on viable opportunities.

2. Segment Your Pipeline:

Categorize leads based on deal size, stage, closing probability, or customer type. This segmentation helps tailor your approach to different groups and prioritize effectively.

3. Use CRM Tools:

Leverage Customer Relationship Management (CRM) tools to automate updates and maintain detailed records of customer interactions. CRM systems can also provide valuable insights and analytics to optimize the pipeline management process.

4. Define Clear Stages:

Clearly define each stage of your sales process, from prospecting to closing. Ensure that the criteria for advancing leads to the next stage are specific and measurable.

5. Monitor Key Metrics:

Track key performance indicators (KPIs) such as conversion rates, average deal size, sales cycle length, and pipeline velocity. Monitoring these metrics can highlight trends and pinpoint areas needing improvement.

6. Focus on High-Quality Leads:

Qualify leads rigorously to ensure your pipeline is filled with opportunities that are more likely to convert. Spend more time nurturing high-quality leads.

7. Regular Reviews:

Conduct regular pipeline reviews with your team to discuss progress and strategize on moving deals forward. Use these reviews as opportunities for coaching and adjusting tactics.

8. Align Sales and Marketing Efforts:

Ensure that your marketing efforts are aligned with your pipeline needs. Regular communication between sales and marketing teams can help generate the correct type of leads and support ongoing deals.

Conclusion

Managing your sales pipeline effectively is a dynamic process that requires continual attention and adjustment. By implementing robust management practices, regularly reviewing performance data, and leveraging technology, you can enhance your pipeline's efficiency and boost your overall sales performance. Effective pipeline management helps achieve sales targets and contributes to sustainable business growth and customer satisfaction.

OVERVIEW OF SALES PLANNING AND ORGANIZATION

Part Seven explores essential sales planning and organization practices, aiming to enhance efficiency, predictability, and success in sales efforts. This section provides a cohesive look at crucial organizational laws, each supplemented with practical exercises and hypothetical scenarios to solidify understanding and application.

Law 31: Stay organized

Core Principle: Maintain an orderly approach to all sales activities to enhance efficiency and effectiveness.

Exercise: Implement a system using digital tools to categorize and prioritize daily tasks, client information, and follow-up reminders.

Hypothetical Scenario: Imagine your database experiencing a glitch and losing recent entries. Develop a contingency plan that ensures you maintain organization and access essential client information without interruption.

Law 32: Practice Effective Time Management

Core Principle: Optimize your daily, weekly, and monthly schedules to maximize productivity and reduce stress.

Exercise: Start each day by scheduling tasks using the time-blocking method and assess the effectiveness of this approach at the end of the week.

Hypothetical Scenario: You are consistently overbooked with meetings, leading to neglected tasks. Reevaluate your schedule to allocate time blocks for core sales activities without over-committing.

Law 33: Set and Review Goals Regularly

Core Principle: Regularly set realistic sales goals and review progress to ensure alignment with overall business objectives.

Exercise: Set specific monthly sales targets and outline steps to achieve these. Use weekly reviews to track progress and make adjustments.

Hypothetical Scenario: Halfway through the quarter, you will likely miss your sales target. Plan a strategy session to identify what can be adjusted immediately to realign with your goals.

Law 34: Prepare for Every Scenario

Core Principle: Anticipate potential challenges in the sales process and prepare strategies to address them.

Exercise: Develop a "scenario plan" that includes potential sales obstacles and document effective responses or solutions to these challenges.

Hypothetical Scenario: Before a significant pitch, a key decision-maker cancels. Prepare an alternative approach to keep the sale on track, either by rescheduling promptly or addressing another critical influencer in the organization.

Law 35: Manage Your Sales Pipeline

Core Principle: Effectively manage and monitor your sales pipeline to ensure a steady flow of prospects and closed deals.

Exercise: Analyze your current sales pipeline for bottlenecks and stages with high drop-off rates. Implement strategies to improve flow and conversion at each stage.

Hypothetical Scenario: Notice a trend where numerous prospects stall at the proposal stage. Investigate underlying causes and develop targeted actions to enhance movement through this critical phase.

Conclusion Of Part Seven

This part of the book equips sales professionals with advanced strategies in planning and organization, essential for sustaining high performance and achieving sales targets. The structured exercises and realistic scenarios help practitioners understand and effectively implement each law in their daily sales activities. By mastering these organizational principles, sales professionals can create a robust framework that supports sustained success and adaptability in a dynamic sales environment.

PART EIGHT: LEVERAGING TECHNOLOGY AND TRENDS

LAW 36: UTILIZE TECHNOLOGY EFFECTIVELY

Technology plays a critical role in every aspect of sales. From customer relationship management (CRM) systems to data analytics and automated marketing tools, effectively utilizing technology can significantly improve efficiency, accuracy, and customer engagement. This law explores the importance of integrating technology into sales processes and guides how to leverage these tools effectively.

Importance Of Technology In Sales

Integrating technology into sales processes offers several key benefits:

1. Enhances Efficiency: Automating routine tasks such as data entry, lead tracking, and follow-ups frees up time for sales professionals to focus on more strategic activities, such as relationship building and closing deals.

2. Improves Accuracy and Consistency: Technology ensures that data is accurately recorded and consistently maintained, reducing the risk of errors with manual handling.

3. Enables Scalability: Technology solutions can quickly scale with your business, supporting increased volumes of sales

activities without a corresponding increase in errors or workload.

4. Provides Valuable Insights: Advanced analytics tools can analyze sales data to identify trends, forecast demand, and provide insights that inform better business decisions.

5. Facilitates Better Customer Engagement: Technology can help personalize customer interactions based on historical data, improving engagement and satisfaction.

Strategies For Effectively Utilizing Technology

To maximize the benefits of technology in sales, consider the following strategies:

1. Choose the Right Tools: Assess your specific needs and challenges and select technology solutions that address these effectively. Whether it's a CRM system, an email marketing tool, or a data analytics platform, the right technology should align with your sales goals and processes.

2. Train Your Team: Ensure all team members are proficient in using the selected technologies. Regular training sessions and updates on new features or tools can help maximize their potential.

3. Integrate Systems: Where possible, integrate your various

technological tools to create a seamless flow of information across platforms. For example, connecting your CRM system to your email platform can automate tracking customer interactions and improve data accuracy.

4. Utilize Mobile Solutions: With the increasing prevalence of remote working, mobile-friendly solutions allow sales teams to access information and perform tasks on the go, increasing responsiveness and flexibility.

5. Regularly Review and Update: Technology evolves rapidly. Regularly review your tech stack to ensure it remains current, efficient, and effective at meeting your business needs. This may involve upgrading existing tools or adopting new technologies as they emerge.

Conclusion

Effectively utilizing technology is no longer optional for sales teams; it is imperative for staying competitive in the modern marketplace. By embracing technological solutions, sales professionals can streamline operations, enhance customer interactions, and achieve better outcomes. The strategic implementation of technology boosts sales efficiency and drives innovation, helping businesses adapt to changing market conditions and customer expectations.

LAW 37: KEEP LEARNING AND EVOLVING

Continuous learning and evolution are not just beneficial; they are essential for long-term success. This law emphasizes ongoing education and adaptation, primarily through learning technologies that streamline learning processes and improve sales proficiency.

The Importance Of Continuous Learning In Sales

Continuous learning in sales is crucial for several reasons:

1. Adapting to Market Changes: The sales environment is dynamic, with frequent shifts in consumer behavior, market conditions, and technology. Continuous learning is the key to staying relevant and practical in such a fast-paced industry.

2. Enhancing Skills and Knowledge: Regular training and education expand a salesperson's skills and knowledge, enabling them to tackle complex challenges and close more deals effectively.

3. Increasing Competitiveness: Staying updated with the latest sales techniques and industry trends is vital for sales professionals to maintain a competitive edge in the market.

4. Promoting Innovation: Learning new approaches and technologies encourages sales professionals to think creatively and improve existing processes, fostering innovation in the industry.

Leveraging Learning Technologies

Learning technologies are indispensable tools and platforms that facilitate the efficient delivery and management of education. Here's how they can be effectively integrated into a sales training program:

1. Online Courses and Webinars: These platforms offer flexible learning opportunities on various sales-related topics, such as negotiation techniques, customer relationship management, and digital marketing, allowing sales professionals to learn at their own pace and on their schedule.

2. Virtual Simulations and Role-Playing: Advanced learning technologies can simulate sales scenarios, providing a risk-free environment for salespeople to practice and hone their skills.

3. Mobile Learning Apps: These apps allow sales professionals to access learning materials on their mobile devices, making learning possible anytime and anywhere, maximizing downtime like commuting or waiting for appointments.

4. Social Learning Platforms: Technologies that enable social learning, such as forums and collaborative platforms,

allow sales professionals to learn from peers and experts in the industry, enhancing knowledge through community engagement.

5. Microlearning Modules: These are short, focused segments of learning designed to teach a specific skill or concept quickly and efficiently, perfect for busy sales professionals looking to enhance a particular aspect of their sales process.

6. YouTube: An invaluable resource for free, diverse content, YouTube offers countless video tutorials, expert talks, and step-by-step guides on virtually every sales aspect, making it an excellent tool for visual learners who benefit from seeing techniques demonstrated in real-time.

Tips For Effective Continuous Learning

1. Set Clear Learning Goals: Identify specific skills or knowledge areas you want to develop and set achievable goals for your learning.

2. Schedule Regular Learning Sessions: Block out time dedicated to learning, treating it as a critical business activity.

3. Apply Learning Immediately: Try to apply new knowledge or skills to real-world sales activities as soon as possible to reinforce learning and gauge effectiveness.

4. Evaluate Progress and Impact: Regularly assess how the new skills or knowledge impact your sales results and adjust your

learning plan accordingly.

5. Encourage a Culture of Learning: If you are in a leadership role, foster an environment that values and encourages continuous learning among all team members.

Conclusion

Keeping up with the rapid evolution of the sales industry demands an ongoing commitment to learning and development. By leveraging modern learning technologies, including YouTube, sales professionals can efficiently and effectively enhance their skills, ensuring they remain at the top of their game and achieve outstanding sales results.

LAW 38: LEVERAGE TRENDS

Staying attuned to and leveraging emerging trends is crucial for maintaining competitiveness and relevance. This law explores the significance of understanding industry trends and how sales professionals can harness these trends to foster innovation, improve customer engagement, and drive sales.

Importance Of Leveraging Trends In Sales

Recognizing and capitalizing on trends is critical for several reasons:

1. Maintain Relevance: Keeping up with trends ensures that your business remains relevant to your customers, who are increasingly informed and influenced by the latest industry developments.

2. Anticipate Market Changes: By understanding trends, you can anticipate changes in the market and adjust your strategies accordingly, staying ahead of competitors who may be slower to adapt.

3. Innovate Proactively: Trends can inspire innovation, providing ideas for new products, services, or improvements that meet evolving customer needs.

4. Enhance Customer Relationships: Demonstrating knowledge of current trends shows customers that you are well informed and proactive, which can strengthen their trust in your ability to serve them effectively.

5. Drive Strategic Decisions: Trend analysis can inform strategic decisions, guiding where to allocate resources, when to expand into new markets, or how to reposition your brand.

Strategies To Leverage Trends Effectively

To maximize the benefits of trends in your sales strategy, consider the following approaches:

1. Regularly Monitor Industry Sources: Stay updated by regularly reading industry publications, attending conferences, and following thought leaders on social media. Tools like Google Alerts can also help track specific topics.

2. Engage with Your Network: Regular interactions with peers, customers, and other industry stakeholders can provide insights into emerging trends and customer sentiments.

3. Analyze Data: Utilize data analytics tools to identify patterns and trends in your sales data and customer feedback. This can help pinpoint emerging demands or shifts in consumer preferences.

4. Experiment with New Approaches: Use insights from trends to experiment with new sales tactics, marketing strategies, or product features. Pilot programs or limited-scale tests can assess the viability of these new ideas.

5. Educate Your Team and Customers: Share your knowledge about trends with your team and customers. For the team, it ensures that everyone is on the same page and can communicate effectively about the latest developments. It adds value to your relationships by positioning you as a trusted customer advisor.

Conclusion

Leveraging trends is not just about following the market—it's about being strategically ahead of the curve. By identifying and acting on emerging trends, sales professionals can adapt to changes and drive growth and innovation within their organizations. This proactive approach ensures continued relevance and success in an ever-evolving market landscape.

LAW 39: UNDERSTAND PRICING STRATEGIES

Pricing is not just a mere reflection of cost but a crucial element of the marketing mix that directly impacts customer perception, competitiveness, and profitability. This law explores various pricing strategies and provides insights into how sales professionals can leverage these strategies to optimize market positioning and sales success.

Importance Of Understanding Pricing Strategies

A thorough understanding of pricing strategies is essential for several reasons:

1. Influences Buying Decisions: Pricing often plays a decisive role in customer purchasing. Effective pricing strategies can attract new customers and retain existing ones.

2. Impacts Profit Margins: The right pricing strategy protects and potentially increases the profit margins by ensuring that the prices cover costs and provide the desired level of profitability.

3. Affects Brand Positioning: How a product is priced affects its market positioning. Premium pricing can position a product as a luxury, while competitive pricing might appeal to cost-conscious buyers.

4. Facilitates Market Entry: For new products, pricing strategies can be used to penetrate the market quickly or slowly build a high-end brand image.

5. Helps in Competing Effectively: Understanding and implementing strategic pricing helps you stay competitive by aligning your offerings with market expectations and competitor pricing.

Key Pricing Strategies

Here are several pricing strategies commonly used in various industries, along with their potential applications:

1. Cost-Plus Pricing: This straightforward strategy involves adding a standard markup to the cost of the product. It's simple to calculate and ensures all costs are covered.

2. Value-Based Pricing: Pricing is based on the perceived value to the customer rather than the cost to produce the product.This strategy can maximize profitability if customers perceive a high value in the offering.

3. Competitive Pricing: Setting prices based on competitors' pricing levels. This strategy is common in highly competitive markets where minor price differences can significantly influence customer decisions.

4. Penetration Pricing: Setting a low price to enter a competitive market and gain market share quickly. The price is typically raised once the initial market entry goals are achieved.

5. Premium Pricing: Setting prices higher than competitors to suggest superior quality and to segment the market. This strategy appeals to status-conscious buyers.

6. Psychological Pricing: Using price points that make a product appear less expensive (e.g., $9.99 instead of $10). This strategy plays a role in customer psychology in increasing sales.

7. Dynamic Pricing: Adjusting prices in real-time based on demand, market conditions, and customer profiles. Common in industries like hospitality and airlines.

Tips For Implementing Effective Pricing Strategies

1. Understand Your Market and Costs: Before setting prices, thoroughly understand your market, including customer expectations and competitive dynamics, as well as your production and delivery costs.

2. Segment Your Market: Tailor your pricing strategies to different customer segments. Different groups may be more sensitive to price changes than others.

3. Monitor and Adapt: The effectiveness of pricing strategies can change over time. Continuously monitor performance and be ready to adjust your pricing to respond to market changes, cost fluctuations, or competitor moves.

4. Communicate Value Effectively: Ensure the value proposition and pricing are communicated. Customers who understand the

value are more likely to accept premium pricing strategies.

Conclusion

Understanding and strategically implementing pricing strategies are crucial for maximizing sales, profitability, and market share. By aligning pricing with overall business strategies and market conditions, sales professionals can influence customer behavior and achieve competitive advantages in the marketplace.

LAW 40: MEASURE YOUR PERFORMANCE

Continuously measuring performance is essential for growth, adaptation, and success. This law outlines the importance of leveraging technology to track and analyze various metrics, such as closing ratios and the effectiveness of different lead sources. It also stresses the need to identify and improve upon weaknesses.

Importance Of Measuring Performance In Sales

Effective performance measurement allows sales professionals to

1. Identify Success Factors: Understand what strategies, techniques, and types of interactions are leading to sales, helping to focus efforts on what works best.

2. Pinpoint Areas for Improvement: Regularly measuring performance highlights weaknesses or areas where sales strategies are not delivering expected results.

3. Enhance Training and Development: Data-driven insights can guide training programs and personal development plans, focusing on areas that will improve sales outcomes.

4. Optimize Resource Allocation: By knowing which activities yield the best ROI, organizations can better allocate resources, whether time, budget, or personnel.

Using Technology To Measure Closing Ratios And Lead Effectiveness

Technology plays a pivotal role in accurately and efficiently measuring sales performance metrics. Here's how it can be applied

1. CRM Systems: Utilize Customer Relationship Management (CRM) systems to track all interactions with prospects and customers, from initial contact to sale closure. These systems can automatically calculate closing ratios by comparing the number of deals closed with the number of opportunities created.

2. Analytics Tools: Advanced analytics tools can dissect closing ratios by dimensions such as lead source, customer demographic, or salesperson. This analysis helps understand which types of leads are most likely to convert, allowing sales teams to focus their efforts more effectively.

3. Automated Reporting: Set up automated reports that regularly provide insights into sales performance. These reports can track trends over time and alert managers to significant performance metrics changes.

Strategies To Measure And Improve Sales Performance

1. Set Clear Metrics: Define clear, quantifiable metrics that reflect your business goals and individual performance targets.

Standard sales metrics include closing ratio, average deal size, and sales cycle length.

2. Regular Reviews: Conduct regular performance reviews using the data collected. These should assess outcomes and evaluate the sales processes and tactics used.

3. Segment Analysis: Break down data by various criteria (e.g., lead source, campaign, team member) to identify which areas are performing well and which are underperforming.

4. Focus on Continuous Improvement: Use performance data to set personal and team goals for continuous improvement. Encourage a culture where feedback is actively sought and used constructively.

5. Leverage Training and Coaching: Based on performance metrics, implement targeted training and coaching sessions to address specific weaknesses or further develop sales team strengths.

Conclusion

Measuring performance is not merely about keeping track of sales numbers; it's about using data to make informed decisions that drive better sales practices. Technology is a crucial enabler in this process, providing the tools necessary to measure, analyze, and ultimately enhance sales performance. By tracking how different leads perform and where there are gaps in skills or processes, sales professionals can systematically improve their results, ensuring sustained success and growth in their careers.

PART NINE: CUSTOMER-CENTRIC SALES

LAW 41: PRIORITIZE CUSTOMER SATISFACTION

Customer satisfaction is the cornerstone of a successful business. It not only fosters loyalty but also enhances reputation through positive word-of-mouth. This law delves into why prioritizing customer satisfaction is essential and provides strategies to ensure that customers are consistently pleased with your products and services.

Importance Of Customer Satisfaction

Focusing on customer satisfaction offers several significant benefits:

1. Encourages Repeat Business: Satisfied customers are more likely to return for additional purchases, reducing the cost and effort required to attract new customers.

2. Enhances Brand Reputation: Positive customer experiences lead to recommendations and referrals, naturally expanding your customer base through the most trusted form of marketing: word-of-mouth.

3. Reduces Customer Churn: High satisfaction levels directly correlate with reduced churn rates, stabilizing revenue streams.

4. Provides Competitive Advantage: In competitive markets, superior customer satisfaction can differentiate your brand and

offer a distinct advantage.

5. Generates Valuable Feedback: Satisfied customers are more engaged and often more willing to provide feedback that can be crucial for continuous improvement.

Strategies To Enhance Customer Satisfaction

To effectively prioritize and enhance customer satisfaction, consider implementing the following strategies:

1. Understand Customer Needs and Expectations: Regularly gather and analyze customer feedback to understand their needs, preferences, and expectations. Use surveys, focus groups, and direct feedback channels to collect this information.

2. Deliver Consistent Quality: Ensure that your products and services consistently meet or exceed the quality standards expected by your customers. Consistency is vital to building trust and satisfaction.

3. Provide Excellent Customer Service: Train your team to handle inquiries, complaints, and feedback professionally and empathetically. Quick, effective resolution of issues is crucial.

4. Personalize Interactions: Tailor your communications and offerings to meet your customers' individual needs. Personalization enhances the customer experience and can significantly boost satisfaction.

5. Implement Loyalty Programs: Create loyalty programs that reward repeat customers with discounts, special offers, or other benefits. These programs not only improve satisfaction but also encourage ongoing business.

6. Monitor and Act on Feedback: Monitor customer feedback and promptly address any issues. Show your customers that their opinions are valued and that their feedback leads to tangible changes.

Conclusion

Prioritizing customer satisfaction is essential for nurturing long-term customer relationships and sustaining business growth. You can ensure high satisfaction by consistently delivering quality products, excellent customer service, and personalized experiences. Regularly assessing customer satisfaction and making it a key metric for your business performance will align your efforts with customer expectations, driving overall success and profitability.

LAW 42: OFFER EXCEPTIONAL CUSTOMER SERVICE

Exceptional customer service goes beyond just providing support. It involves creating memorable, engaging, personalized experiences that build customer loyalty and set your brand apart. This approach offers innovative strategies to enhance your service delivery, ensuring that every customer interaction is outstanding.

To Transform Basic Service Into Exceptional Experiences, Consider The Following Strategies:

1. Create Seamless Multi-Channel Support: Enable customers to reach you through various channels and ensure consistent, high-quality service across all platforms.

2. Develop a Proactive Service Culture: Train your team to anticipate and address customer needs before they become issues.

3. Implement a Customer Loyalty Feedback Loop: Establish a direct line of communication for loyal customers to share their needs and suggestions.

4. Customize Customer Interactions Using Data Analytics:

Use data analytics to deeply understand customer behaviors and preferences and tailor your communications and offers accordingly.

5. Empower Customers Through Self-Service: Provide robust self-service options like detailed FAQs and video tutorials.

6. Celebrate Customer Milestones: Acknowledge and celebrate important milestones in your customers' journey with your brand.

7. Focus on Emotional Intelligence Training: Train your customer service team in emotional intelligence skills to better understand and respond to customers' emotional states.

By implementing these innovative customer service strategies, your business can exceed customer expectations, build lasting loyalty, and differentiate itself in the market, ultimately driving sustainable growth and customer satisfaction.

LAW 43: EDUCATE YOUR CUSTOMERS

Educating your customers transcends traditional sales pitches and fosters an environment where knowledge sharing creates value for both the customer and your business. This law explores how proactive customer education can be a game-changer in how customers engage with your products and brand.

Why Customer Education Is A Game Changer

Educating customers beyond simple product knowledge involves engaging customers with deep insights into the industry, their challenges, and innovative solutions. Here's why it's crucial:

1. Creates Informed Advocates: Educated customers understand the finer points of your products and the problems they solve, turning them into advocates who can convincingly share their experiences with others.

2. Differentiates Your Brand: By providing exceptional learning experiences, you differentiate your brand as a leader in customer empowerment and support, not just a product or service provider.

3. Drives Product Innovation: Feedback from well-informed customers is often more insightful, helping to drive innovation and improvements that are finely tuned to market needs.

Innovative Strategies To Educate Your Customers

To elevate the educational experience, consider these innovative strategies:

1. Interactive Learning Tools: Develop interactive tools such as configurators, simulators, or immersive tutorials that allow customers to learn by doing, providing a hands-on understanding of your products or services.

2. Community-Driven Learning: Foster a community where customers can learn from each other, share experiences, and solve problems collectively. This can be facilitated through forums, user groups, or social media platforms.

3. Gamification: Introduce gamification elements in educational content to make learning about your products or industry fun and engaging. Rewards for completing educational challenges can increase participation and retention of information.

4. Storytelling Techniques: Use storytelling to frame educational content, making complex information more accessible and relatable. Stories can illustrate real-life applications of your products or services, memorably highlighting their value.

5. Regular Educational Updates: Keep your customers informed about the latest developments in your product line and the industry. This can be done through newsletters, podcasts, or regular webinars, ensuring customers feel continually supported and valued.

6. Tailored Education Paths: Recognize customers' learning needs and preferences. Offer tailored educational paths that customers can choose based on their expertise level or specific interests.

Conclusion

By prioritizing customer education, you do more than inform—you engage customers meaningfully, enhancing their experience and loyalty. Effective education turns your customer base into knowledgeable partners who deeply understand and value your offerings, which is instrumental in building lasting relationships and driving sustainable growth.

LAW 44: UTILIZE CUSTOMER FEEDBACK

Utilizing customer feedback effectively is pivotal for incremental improvements and driving transformative changes within your organization. This law focuses on innovative and actionable strategies to extract, analyze, and implement customer feedback to enhance product offerings, customer service, and strategic decision-making.

Strategic Importance Of Customer Feedback

Customer feedback is more than a metric of satisfaction—it's a direct line of communication that can inform strategic decisions:

1. Direct Product Improvements: Feedback can provide specific insights into what features or aspects of your products need refinement or enhancement.

2. Guide Innovation: Customer suggestions often contain seeds of innovative ideas that can lead to new product development or services.

3. Cultural Impact: A culture that embraces customer feedback strengthens internal commitment to customer-centricity, enhancing all areas of operation.

Dynamic Ways To Utilize Customer Feedback

Here are advanced strategies to elevate how your organization uses customer feedback:

1. Integrate Feedback into Product Development Cycles: Use customer insights as regular input for product development meetings to ensure your build meets user expectations and needs.

2. Real-Time Feedback Systems: Implement real-time feedback tools that allow customers to comment on their experiences as they occur. For instance, digital kiosks, mobile apps, or quick online surveys immediately post-service can capture impressions when they're most vivid.

3. Feedback-Driven Training Programs: Design training sessions for customer service and product teams based on common feedback themes. This aligns team development with actual customer experiences and expectations.

4. Advanced Analytical Tools: Utilize machine learning algorithms to analyze feedback for sentiment, emerging patterns, and hidden insights that might be overlooked through manual processes.

5. Feedback Transparency: Share feedback publicly where appropriate—such as product reviews and testimonials on your website—to demonstrate transparency and build trust with potential customers.

Conclusion

Effectively utilizing customer feedback requires a structured approach beyond merely collecting data—it involves embedding insights into the fabric of your organization's strategy. By actively seeking and thoughtfully applying customer input, businesses can create more relevant products, deliver superior service, and ultimately build a loyal customer base.

LAW 45: ENHANCE CUSTOMER EXPERIENCE

Creating a standout customer experience is critical in today's competitive marketplace. It's not just about meeting expectations but consistently exceeding them in memorable and impactful ways. Here's how you can improve the customer experience in simple yet effective ways.

Focused Strategies To Directly Improve Customer Experience

1. Direct Feedback Opportunities: Implement real-time feedback mechanisms where customers can express their satisfaction or dissatisfaction during the interaction. This immediate loop allows for on-the-spot adjustments to enhance their experience.

2. Moment of Surprise: Integrate a 'moment of surprise' in your regular customer interactions, such as a small gift at the end of a purchase or a personalized thank you note written on the spot. This small gesture can leave a big impression.

3. Speed of Service: Focus intensely on reducing wait times and speeding up service delivery. Fast, efficient service respects the customer's time and significantly enhances their perception of your brand.

4. Simplification of Processes: Simplify any necessary paperwork or procedures that customers need. Making processes more accessible and less time-consuming can improve the overall customer experience.

5. Personalized Recommendations: Use brief interactions to gather information about customer preferences and provide personalized recommendations. This shows attentiveness and can make the customer feel uniquely valued.

Conclusion

These strategies are designed to provide a straightforward yet powerful impact on how customers perceive their interactions with your brand. Focusing on these critical areas ensures that each customer leaves with a positive impression, driven by efficiency, personal attention, and unexpected delights.

OVERVIEW OF CUSTOMER-CENTRIC SALES

Part Nine emphasizes adopting a customer-centric approach in sales, detailing strategies prioritizing customer satisfaction, engagement, and overall experience. Each law is accompanied by practical exercises and hypothetical scenarios designed to enhance understanding and apply these strategies.

Law 41: Prioritize Customer Satisfaction

Core Principle: Ensure customer satisfaction is at the forefront of all business operations.

Exercise: Conduct a monthly customer satisfaction survey and analyze the results to identify areas for improvement.

Hypothetical Scenario: A customer has reported dissatisfaction with a recent purchase. Develop a response plan that addresses the issue, rectifies the situation, and turns the customer's experience around, demonstrating your commitment to satisfaction.

Law 42: Offer Exceptional Customer Service

Core Principle: Deliver service beyond the basics to delight customers truly.

Exercise: Role-play complex customer service scenarios with

your team to refine their problem-solving and communication skills.

Hypothetical Scenario: A loyal customer encounters a rare product defect. Script out a service response that resolves the issue efficiently and reinforces the customer's loyalty through exceptional service.

Law 43: Educate Your Customers

Core Principle: Use every opportunity to inform and educate customers, enhancing their ability to make informed decisions.

Exercise: Create informational brochures or an online knowledge base that helps customers understand your products better.

Hypothetical Scenario: A potential customer is considering your product alongside competitors. Prepare an educational session highlighting your product's unique benefits without directly disparaging your competitors.

Law 44: Utilize Customer Feedback

Core Principle: Actively seek out and implement feedback to improve your products and services.

Exercise: Set up a feedback loop using customer surveys, direct calls, and digital feedback tools. Regularly review the feedback in team meetings and implement actionable changes.

Hypothetical Scenario: Feedback indicates that several customers find one aspect of your software challenging. Plan a strategy to address these usability concerns in the next software update.

Law 45: Enhance Customer Experience

Core Principle: Continuously find new ways to enhance the overall customer experience, ensuring it remains positive and engaging.

Exercise: Map the customer journey to identify and improve potential friction points.

Hypothetical Scenario: Notice a trend where customers drop off at a particular sales funnel stage. Investigate and devise a plan to enhance the experience at this specific point to increase conversion rates.

Conclusion Of Part Nine

This part of the book empowers sales professionals to embrace a customer-centric approach, which is crucial for building lasting relationships and achieving sustained success. The exercises and scenarios help practitioners understand and apply each law effectively, fostering a culture prioritizing customer well-being and satisfaction.

PART TEN: HEALTH AND SUSTAINABILITY IN SALES

LAW 46: MAINTAIN A HIGH ENERGY LEVEL

High energy levels in sales invigorate your sales approach and communicate enthusiasm and confidence to customers, significantly impacting their buying decisions. This law outlines why maintaining a high energy level is crucial and provides strategies to sustain it throughout your sales activities.

Importance Of High Energy Levels In Sales

1. Enhances Engagement: High energy is contagious and can elevate the customer's mood and engagement level during interactions.

2. Build Confidence: In both yourself and the customer's eyes, displaying high energy often translates to competence and enthusiasm for your product.

3. Increases Productivity: Higher energy levels increase productivity and the ability to handle demanding sales days more effectively.

Tips To Maintain High Energy Levels

Here are practical tips to ensure you consistently maintain high energy during your sales activities:

1. Regular Exercise: Incorporate regular physical activity or walks into your routine. Exercise boosts your overall energy levels and improves mood and mental clarity.

2. Balanced Diet: Focus on a nutritious diet that stabilizes energy throughout the day. Include slow-releasing energy foods like whole grains and proteins, and avoid heavy meals that can lead to energy slumps.

3. Adequate Hydration: Dehydration can cause fatigue and decreased alertness. Ensure you drink enough water throughout the day to keep your energy levels up.

4. Sufficient Sleep: Prioritize getting enough sleep each night. Lack of sleep can severely impact your energy levels, mood, and ability to concentrate.

5. Strategic Caffeine Use: Use caffeine strategically to boost your energy levels before low periods in the day. Be cautious not to overconsume, as it can lead to crashes or affect your sleep.

6. Energy Management Techniques: Learn and practice energy management techniques such as deep breathing exercises, short meditative breaks, or power naps when possible to recharge quickly.

7. Positive Interactions: Engage in positive interactions with colleagues and customers. Positive emotions are linked to higher energy levels.

8. Organize and Prioritize: Reduce stress and feeling overwhelmed by organizing your tasks and focusing on one thing at a time. Stress can drain your energy more than physical tiredness.

Conclusion

Maintaining a high energy level is crucial for sales professionals, influencing how they feel and customers perceive them. By adopting these strategies, you can ensure that your energy levels support your goals to be an effective and successful salesperson.

LAW 47: AVOID BURNOUT

Burnout can significantly impair productivity and enthusiasm, particularly in high-stress professions like sales. This law provides essential tips on preventing burnout and effectively responding if you start feeling overwhelmed.

Importance Of Avoiding Burnout

Burnout affects your mental and physical health and impacts your job performance and customer relationships. Preventing burnout is crucial for maintaining long-term career success and personal well-being.

Strategies To Prevent Burnout Here Are Proactive Steps To Avoid Burnout In The Sales Environment:

1. Set Clear Boundaries: Establish and maintain clear boundaries between work and personal life. This could mean setting specific work hours and sticking to them, or learning to say no to non-essential tasks that can be delegated or postponed.

2. Take Regular Breaks: Take short breaks to step away from your work throughout the day. A five-minute walk or stretching can help clear your mind and reduce stress.

3. Prioritize Tasks: Use prioritization methods like the Eisenhower Box to distinguish between urgent and important tasks. Focusing on what truly matters can reduce feelings of being overwhelmed.

4. Develop a Support Network: Building a network of colleagues, friends, and family who understand the demands of your job and can provide support is crucial. Sharing your experiences with peers can also provide new insights or validation of your challenges, making you feel less alone in your journey.

5. Engage in Regular Physical Activity: Regular exercise relieves stress. Whether it's a gym session, yoga, or a daily walk, find an activity you enjoy and make it a part of your routine.

6. Practice Mindfulness and Relaxation Techniques: Meditation, deep breathing exercises, or progressive muscle relaxation can significantly lower stress levels and help maintain mental health.

7. Pursue Hobbies and Interests Outside of Work: Engage in activities that make you happy and aren't related to work. This can not only improve your mood but also recharge your batteries.

What To Do If You Feel Burnt Out

If you start to feel burnout setting in, it's essential to take immediate steps to address it:

1. Acknowledge the Feelings: Recognize and acknowledge that you are experiencing burnout. Understanding that it's a common issue can help you address it without guilt or stigma.

2. Adjust Your Workload: Discuss your workload with your manager and explore possible adjustments. Sometimes, redistributing or prioritizing different tasks can make a significant difference.

3. Take Time Off: Take a short break or vacation to disconnect entirely from work. This can provide you with the distance needed to recharge fully.

Conclusion

Preventing and managing burnout is essential for sustaining a successful and fulfilling career in sales. By implementing these strategies, you can remain energetic, motivated, and effective in your role while maintaining your health and well-being.

LAW 48: EMBRACE THE JOURNEY OF CONSTANT GROWTH!

Continuous improvement in sales equips professionals with the necessary tools and mindset to adapt, thrive, and succeed in a dynamic environment. This law outlines robust strategies for integrating lifelong learning and development into your daily sales practices.

Why Continuous Improvement Is Essential

Continuous improvement helps sales professionals adapt to changing markets, enhance effectiveness, unlock new professional opportunities, and maintain personal career engagement.

Enhanced Strategies For Continuous Improvement

Here are detailed strategies to deeply integrate continuous improvement into your sales career

1. Set Specific Learning Goals:

Actionable Strategy: Identify critical areas for development and set SMART goals to ensure focused and measurable progress.

Example: If your goal is to improve customer relationship management, commit to mastering a new CRM software, attending a related seminar, and applying these skills with at least 30 customers over the next quarter.

2. Regular Training and Education:

Actionable Strategy: Continually invest in your education through formal courses, workshops, and self-study. Utilize both online platforms and in-person events to keep your skills sharp.

Example: Enroll in quarterly workshops focused on advanced sales techniques and supplement this with monthly webinars on industry trends.

3. Reflective Practice

Actionable Strategy: Establish a routine of reflecting on your sales experiences to identify effective strategies and areas for improvement.

Example: After each sales interaction, take time to jot down key points in a sales journal, focusing on what went well and what could be improved. Review this journal monthly to devise adjustments.

4. Read and Research:

Actionable Strategy: Regularly dedicate time to reading books and industry publications to gain insights into sales strategies and customer psychology.

Example: Maintain a curated list of must-read books for the year and set aside an hour each week for reading. Share insights with peers to reinforce understanding and application.

5. Use Technology and Journals to Track Progress:

Actionable Strategy: Employ digital tools and maintain a detailed journal to track your professional development and the impact of new strategies on your sales performance.

Example: Use a digital dashboard to visualize progress on learning goals and complement this with a handwritten journal to record insights, reflections, and personal milestones in your continuous learning journey.

Conclusion

Adopting a continuous improvement mindset involves actively seeking knowledge, applying innovative practices, and critically assessing outcomes. By methodically enhancing your skills and adjusting based on feedback and results, you ensure ongoing growth and sustained success in your sales career.

FINAL CHAPTER: THE SYMPHONY OF SALES SUCCESS

Success is not achieved through isolated actions but through a symphony of interconnected strategies and principles. This final chapter synthesizes the 48 laws presented in this book, illustrating how they collectively forge a robust and adaptive approach to mastering the sales process.

Interconnection and Synergy of the Laws

Each law we've explored is critical in the larger composition of sales excellence. Each note has its strength when played alone, but when harmonized with others, a full melody emerges that is richer and more compelling. Here's how these laws interlink and support each other:

1. Foundation and Growth: Laws focused on foundational skills, such as understanding your product and knowing your customer, set the stage for more advanced techniques like negotiation and closing deals. Mastery of the basics ensures that when more complex situations arise, you are well-prepared to handle them with sophistication and depth.

2. Continuous Feedback and Improvement: The continuous cycle of feedback (Law 44) and improvement (Law 48) is a recurring theme that enhances every other law. By constantly

applying these principles, sales professionals can refine their approach in real-time, ensuring their methods are as effective as possible.

3. Customer-Centric Strategies: Laws emphasizing customer satisfaction, service, and experience (Laws 41-45) are deeply interconnected. They stress the importance of viewing every interaction through the lens of customer impact, ensuring that the strategies employed meet and exceed customer expectations.

4. Adaptation and Innovation: The laws encouraging ongoing education and adaptation to market trends (Laws 37 and 48) support the need for sales professionals to be agile and forward-thinking. This readiness not only prepares you to adjust to changes but also to drive innovation within your industry.

5. Personal Development and Performance: At the heart of many laws is the focus on personal development, whether through enhancing presentation skills, managing time efficiently, or maintaining high energy levels. These personal competencies are crucial as they directly influence every sales interaction and overall career trajectory.

Conclusion: A Cohesive Strategy For Sales Mastery

As we conclude this journey through the 48 sales laws, it is clear that the path to sales mastery is not linear but cyclical and interconnected. Each law does not stand alone but is a thread in a larger tapestry. Sales professionals who embrace these interconnected principles will find themselves not just succeeding in isolated moments but thriving consistently over the long term.

The actual effectiveness of your approach lies not just in mastering individual techniques but in how these techniques are integrated and executed together. As you continue to apply and integrate these laws into your daily sales practices, you will develop a comprehensive strategy that is dynamic, adaptive, and ultimately successful.

BOOKS BY THIS AUTHOR

Cracking The Code: The Formula For Closing Deals

Unlock the ultimate guide to mastering the art of closing deals with "Cracking the Code: The Formula for Closing Deals." This comprehensive handbook provides a systematic approach to navigating the complexities of sales with confidence and precision.

From understanding the prospect's needs to skillfully addressing objections and sealing the deal, each chapter unveils practical strategies and actionable insights essential for achieving unparalleled success in sales. Whether you're a seasoned sales professional or an aspiring entrepreneur, this book equips you with the tools and techniques needed to elevate your sales game and unlock new opportunities.

With real-world examples, exercises, and proven techniques, "Cracking the Code" empowers you to cultivate meaningful relationships with prospects, deliver value-driven solutions, and confidently close deals. Get ready to revolutionize your approach to sales and achieve extraordinary results with the powerful formula revealed within these pages.

Saving Sammy: A Kids Guide To Finaical Litercy

Saving Sammy is a fun and engaging book that teaches kids the importance of financial literacy.

Through the story of a young boy named Sammy, readers will

learn about budgeting, saving, and spending wisely. Sammy loves to play video games and eat junk food, but when he realizes that he never has enough money to buy the things he really wants, he decides to make a change. With the help of his parents, friends and new financial skills, Sammy learns how to set goals, make a budget, and save for what he really wants.

This book is perfect for kids who want to learn about money management in a fun and engaging way.

Dollars And Sense: A Kids Money Guide

Step into the magical world of Sammy as he embarks on a fun journey of financial discovery in "Dollars and Sense: A Kids' Money Guide." This captivating book is designed to make learning about money exciting. Sammy's story unfolds with real-life money-saving strategies, clever tips, and tricks that will inspire the genius entrepreneur within every young mind. Through vibrant illustrations and engaging storytelling, children will be drawn into Sammy's world of imagination, where they'll learn valuable skills to turn their creative ideas into profitable money-making ventures.

At every turn, young readers will encounter exciting saving challenges that transform the concept of money management into a wild adventure. From thrilling scavenger hunts to creative money-making games, they'll discover the magic of saving, all while having a blast with Sammy.

But the journey doesn't stop there! Sammy believes in celebrating success, and readers will witness his triumphs as he throws a spectacular party of saving achievements. This celebration showcases the power of financial responsibility and the joy of reaching savings goals.

Hundred Dollar Hustle: Blueprint

For A Profitable Business

At a time when big dreams often come with even more significant price tags, this blueprint stands out. "The $100 Hustle Blueprint for a Profitable Business" invites you to embark on an extraordinary journey from a $100 budget to entrepreneurial success! This extraordinary book provides secrets for turning scarcity into profit, adversity into resilience, and $100 into a flourishing enterprise. Through these pages, you'll also learn the art of thinking beyond boundaries; constraints will only serve to foster creativity! Be amazed as you discover the power of your unique vision, where innovation is an ever-present compass to lead you forward in uncharted territory. "The $100 Hustle Blueprint" explores how listening to your target audience, mastering market research on a budget, and creating an effective business plan can all lead to realizing your dreams. Prepare to embark on an incredible adventure where every dollar saved becomes an investment in your dream. Explore the DIY branding and marketing world, where authenticity and passion are your most effective marketing weapons. Take steps towards developing customer relationships so one-time buyers become lifelong fans! As you read, you will learn to embrace challenges as opportunities, viewing each obstacle as an essential building block toward success. By finishing this book, you will know how to build a sustainable and enduring business to thrive in today's ever-evolving entrepreneurial landscape. "The $100 Hustle Blueprint" can guide you on an extraordinary journey where success doesn't simply depend on numbers; its meaning lies in creating positive impacts, touching lives, and leaving a legacy behind. Join the visionary entrepreneurs who dared to dream, innovate, and turn $100 into an empire. Your adventure awaits in these pages; let the world experience your $100 hustle!

www.ingramcontent.com/pod-product-compliance
Lightning Source LLC
Chambersburg PA
CBHW050207230526
45470CB00001B/282